About the Author

Dermoth Alexander Henry, known as The Scribe, has a lot to thank his Creator for, knowing that his Creator has blessed him as a wordsmith. He has wonderful parents which has made The Scribe's journey easy. After writing his last book *Liberators* writing this book has become a great achievement.

Dermoth Alexander Henry - The Scribe

THE GHOST WITHIN

AUSTIN MACAULEY PUBLISHERS™
LONDON · CAMBRIDGE · NEW YORK · SHARJAH

Copyright © Dermoth Alexander Henry (2018)

The right of Dermoth Alexander Henry to be identified as author of this work has been asserted by him in accordance with section 77 and 78 of the Copyright, Designs and Patents Act 1988.

All rights reserved. No part of this publication may be reproduced, stored in a retrieval system, or transmitted in any form or by any means, electronic, mechanical, photocopying, recording, or otherwise, without the prior permission of the publishers.

Any person who commits any unauthorized act in relation to this publication may be liable to criminal prosecution and civil claims for damages.

A CIP catalogue record for this title is available from the British Library.

ISBN 9781786297877 (Paperback)
ISBN 9781786297884 (Hardback)
ISBN 9781786297891 (E-Book)

www.austinmacauley.com

First Published (2018)
Austin Macauley Publishers Ltd™
25 Canada Square
Canary Wharf
London
E14 5LQ

Dedication

I would be justified in saying the Creator is my inspiration and by life, I'm inspired to write.

This book is dedicated to my brother Carlton Henry, my mother Belzie Deloris Henry, my father Joseph Brian Henry and my sister Joan Adassa Henry who have sadly passed away. Their memories will always be with me, for they have gone to the realms unseen.

Now I'm also thanking all the other people that have helped me develop my skills from poetry to fiction to non-fiction. Also, for people that have read my work and have given me the encouragement, to go ahead and write another book.

DERMOTH ALEXANDER HENRY

KNOWN AS THE SCRIBE

CHAPTER 1

This book isn't about what's wrong and what's right, it's about me introducing to you your inner man or woman, who I call our Ghosts. The reason why I haven't called the book The Spirit that lays within you is that our Ghosts and the spirit are two different entities and they play separate roles in our lives. Your spirit, which acts in combination with the flesh, can determine what you're going to do next, that only applies if with your Ghost, you're not in communication with the ELEDA.

Let me just introduce you to (ELEDA MI, which means 'my creator', in the African language Yoruba, who is (ICALABORA) the Self-Existent One.

Neither is this book about you calling the creator ELEDA or saying that ICALABORA is the Self-Existent One. The book is about you understanding who is, and because the Self-Existent One is, this world cannot contain the ELEDA'S unfathomable wisdom.

I would like you to take time out to understand the difference between a title and a name. Every man, woman and child has many a titles and as we are born the first title we're given is 'baby' and then 'child'. Then we have another title called boy or girl' and steadily as we grow up we become teenagers. Until one day we ourselves become parents and not forgetting siblings, nieces, uncles, grandparents and great grandparents.

All those that I've mentioned above are titles and to stress my point, even animals have more than two titles. Each of these; titles that I have described above as people have a name It could be an African name as well as an Asian name or a Russian name, they all possess a name yet they have many titles. As for the ELEDA, which means 'creator', he has but one title and that is creator, and from this word branches off 'the Self-Existent-One', which in turn means 'creator' and ICALABORA is the name given, existing through no means of procreation. Thus ICALABORA becomes the Self-Existent One, likewise meaning 'creator'.

I want you to notice that I never call ICALABORA 'him' or 'being' or 'higher power', but I choose my words very carefully and with delicacy, as I caress the words with love, I will entertain your mind to an ecstatic joy while you weigh up, the many reasons why I will not compromise but show you the fact that I've found ICALABORA whom I've been looking for.

The Ghost in us has one identity and that is to deal with ICALABORA. The ELEDA'S entity is of the beyond and no human can comprehend the things that the ELEDA can achieve; neither can they determine the next move the Self-Existent One makes.

Being a preacher of a gospel that I now know as strange to me, has also helped me to grasp reality by the horns and know that I will never accept any man's truth but that which has being given to me by the ELEDA. To understand the unfathomable depths of the Self-Existent One is amazing, just to get the full comprehension of how the ELEDA deals with us.

With our flesh we serve two masters, which is the dual combination between one and the same spirit good and evil. Yet with our Ghost we're dedicated to pleasing the ELEDA (creator). While the Ghost has more depth and intellect, now, than the flesh, there was a point in the flesh's existence that it would have had the same intellect. Let me explain myself clearly while I break it down for you. When a man or woman's Ghost was created it was created perfect. In the transformation between the Ghost and the flesh, the same goes for the flesh being made perfect in the transformation. Now the flesh, unlike the Ghost was made but, and I repeat but, the Ghost was created. In the earliest form of man's survival because their flesh was made perfect and their intellect intact, they had command over great achievements like the pyramids in Africa.

There is a life beyond which we can comprehend and that is the abode where the ELEDA (creator) has set he's domain. His intelligence is far beyond the imaginations of man's concepts, above and below. Only our Ghosts; has entry to this domain because the communication is between the ELEDA and our Ghost.

Understand this: that the packages came in two bundles but the first bundle was created and the second bundle was made. That gives the first bundle predominance over the second. Now the third bundle was a by-product of the second bundle. The third bundle is the spirit and the second is the flesh while the first is the Ghost.

Now because the first was created, it finds no peace with the second that was made and because the third is a by-product of the second, the second and the third would cleave together to make war against the first that was created. I'm going to ask you a question, if you could show jealousy towards somebody you don't even know, then why couldn't your spirit be jealous of your inner man or woman whom I call your Ghosts?

What we refuse to understand is the fact that it is the spirit that sees someone and immediately shows signs of jealousy, or how do you explain the fact that they don't know that person yet their behavior is so unkind?

It's the spirit that influences the flesh to do the deeds that the flesh craves. I just want to say that I'm fifty-five years old and for me to get it right, I'm humbled by this book because things I never knew the ELEDA is revealing to me as I write each page. Now the difference between the Ghost that dwells in a man and a spirit is that a spirit has two entities, good and evil, and these two entities branch off into a multitude of different ways. Like you could be good to your children and good to your parents and friends, yet you discriminate against your neighbors because of the colour of their skin or the country they come from. When talking about that, the same mouth that a husband takes and kisses his wife with he will in turn curse his children and vice versa with her. That is what you call two entities of the same spirit or dual personality of the spirit.

Can you imagine our spirit that has been tainted by corruption being with the ELEDA for eternity? I didn't think you could.

It is one and the same spirit that is in operation in us that tells us good and evil. Have you ever heard yourself say too a friend and I quote from our mouths, "I (shouldn't) tell you this (but")? This is what I'm saying about the duel side of the spirits personality. And again they call it white lies and black lies, but it's simple both lies that stem from one of the duel sides of the spirit.

How do I define spirit? Well imagine if you were about to make a cup of tea for yourself. You would most certainly need a cup, teabag, milk and sugar. Now let's use symbolic terminology, the cup would represent the Self-Existent One enclosing us roundabout and securing us from danger while comforting us when nobody cares. The teabag would be your Ghost which has direct dealings with the creator. Because the Self-Existent One knew us before we became flesh and has love for us ELEDA MI will show interest in us. The ELEDA gives us milk to have strong bones which stands for all the religious stages that we all went through, until we've found the Self-Existent One who we've searched for. Now the sugar and the water, when diluted, go together. They represent the dual personality of one and the same spirit: good and evil. Just like we know that water is good for us, we also know that sugar is bad for you and feeds on cancerous cells. That explains the spirit and its dual ability to perform. Although being sweet it becomes sour.

Now I'm going to give you an example but please, I would like you to read this with understanding. A man holds fifty people hostage and then he sporadically empties his gun into the crowd of people, thus killing twenty and wounding ten. His next intention is to become a suicide bomber with the remaining thirty people. I know this example takes it to the extreme but I just want to show you the capability of the spirit and the flesh and how detrimental they are. With the flesh and the spirit combined it determined that man's end and other innocent people were killed because of that man's dual combination of spirit and flesh.

That example was given because this kind of act is a reality, just like I say that you could be good to your friends and family yet you discriminate against your neighbors. I'm just trying to show you the dual personality of the same spirit: good and evil.

Our Ghost is not someone to be spooked over because your Ghost existed before the flesh that you occupy. What man refuses to understand is that before he or she appeared on the scene, they were masked with the ELEDA in the form of their Ghosts and that, my friend, allowed the ELEDA to know us and all our shortcomings. The difference between the ELEDA and us is that the ELEDA can see way into the future of any one man, woman or child because of the fact that we existed way back when with the ELEDA (creator.)

The Self-Existent One doesn't need a representative to speak or expose the work that the ELEDA does. Think about it: if ICALABORA created the tongue then the creator must know how to speak, even if it's in the heart of man. ICALABORA does communicate but man today refuses to hear.

To exercise telepathy with the ELEDA is the easiest step to take because this is one of the many ways that the ELEDA actually deals with us. How do we define telepathy? Well, it's easy! Telepathy is the communication of two sources or more with telepathic wavelengths. It runs like a flowing river and the breaking down of unseen barriers. Telepathy isn't necessarily hearing a voice; it is more of an action or a response to a direct command. Our Ghosts are so advanced in their response to ELEDA'S invisible unseeing wavelengths of communication, which within themselves are unfathomable. If the ELEDA created all the universes and all we see and don't, then what's to say that the ELEDA can't deal with the inner man or woman?

When my mother was alive and had settled down in Jamaica I would always talk to her on the phone. It's like ICALABORA when communicating with people as if the word cometh throughout eternity and reaches us at the appointed period. The only difference is when the ELEDA is dealing with you and somebody else is on the phone. When the ELEDA speaks there is no getting your wires crossed, there is no long conversation and because the ELEDA is dealing with your Ghost, the message is written on the template of your heart. The ELEDA is straight forward and to the point: no procrastinating.

To tell the truth whenever the ELEDA speaks to you by telepathy I would liken it to a direct communication between humans that know little about themselves and the qualities that they possess.

Your Ghost has the capability to deal directly with the ELEDA. I hope that you know where I'm going with this because no middle man is needed, thus leaving a direct link between you and the creator.

Know this: the Ghost that lays within you is the key to unlocking and capturing parts of the unfathomable truths of the ELEDA.

The struggles between the Ghost and the spirit are tremendous because the spirit moves hand in hand with the flesh and what the flesh strives for, in many cases so does the spirit and vice versa. So a person doesn't become addicted only because of the flesh but also the spirit. Now the spirit can't determine good from evil because it has two entities of the same spirit. I can only give you this example and hope it will suffice: you could want something so bad knowing that it's no good for you, yet because of the determination of the spirit and the flesh there is no room for you to hear the Ghost within you.

You may suffer from diabetes and your doctor tells you that if you don't give up taking too much sugar you're going to die. The flesh doesn't want to die but it is the spirit that craves the sugar. Another example is: you could have cancer through smoking and you go to your doctor and he tells you that you have to give up smoking immediately. Now your flesh wants to give it up but your spirit is addicted and so it goes for alcohol and drugs!

As I said, because the spirit and the flesh strive together it is the spirit that suggests to the flesh, under the guise that the flesh is doing a good thing, to get addicted to something that is detrimental to all, that take it.

ICALABORA knows exactly what we need, when you need it and how much to give us. It doesn't necessarily have to be material wealth. Yes, it could be that the ELEDA is dealing with your Ghost on a higher level, that when you speak people take note and because of you they change their pattern of thought. The quality of the Ghost that lays within you has boundaries beyond the moon, the sun, the stars, the cosmos and the galaxies.

Now the difference between the Ghost and the spirit, with the Ghost there is perfect democracy and dialog, whether by visions or personal reasoning. ICALABORA will show interest in you. I will give you an example: Twenty-seven years ago ICALABORA said to me, "Show me your hands." But it wasn't until seventeen years ago that I realized that the ELEDA wanted me to start writing. What I'm trying to show you is that the Self-Existent One perceived this day some twenty-seven years ago.

No matter what age you are, before you chose this book the Self-Existent One knew you would choose it. Even before your great-grandparents were conceived, ICALABORA knew that you would be who you are and the interests you would have. Don't get me wrong it's about the interest that the ELEDA has shown in you since your conception. We all get it wrong in life, that is why our Ghosts there to help us to put it right.

Talking about the Ghost, or if you prefer the inner man or the inner woman, we should all know that we can't see the Ghost that lays within us. As for the spirit, in most cases your facial expression will manifest what or how your spirit is feeling. That just goes to prove how the flesh and spirit go hand in hand.

Your inner man or woman, which I call your Ghost, has many attributes and here I will take the time out to explain. Many moons ago me my step-son and his friend were playing a game of monopoly, it was my turn on the dice and to capitalize on my money I would need to throw eleven on the dice to get to free parking. Having more than a strong feeling about this, I asked the ELEDA whether I should gamble and the reply was simply, "Yes." At this point I had enough confidence to strike up a deal with them. The deal was that I give them each three hundred pounds and if eleven comes up they give me six hundred pounds each. I would like you to remember that you only get one chance to throw a six and five. After that my game would be all over. But what I must also remind you is that to throw six and five on the dice I would have to be specific; it's not like throwing five and two to get seven or four and three to also get seven.

On every other throw of the dice, except twelve and eleven, you get two choices of numbers or sometimes three. For instance if you wanted nine on the, dice you could have six and three or five and four. Both of them add up to nine but they are different numbers. To cut a long story short I got the eleven on the dice and I also got the money that was in the middle from free parking.

While you try to fathom why I told you this story, well to tell you the truth this was just a game and how the ELEDA deals with us. What I'm trying to show you is that this follows us in life.

There are times when the ELEDA does something in our lives that we don't understand and, to tell the truth, we would question the ELEDA and even blame the Self-Existent One for our shortcomings. Let me let you into a little secret. The Self-Existent One, no matter what we're going through, designed the act upon our life so that we, in the long run, would be closer and responsive towards the one who created us. The only advice I can give you in this situation is to humble yourself before the ELEDA humbles you and because ICALABORA loves you, the Self-Existent One wants us to abide in the same domain where the Self-Existent One lives.

ICALABORA has always shown me, in my religious experiences, that faith isn't blind but it is tangible. You can either feel touch, smell, hear or see the results. Just like in the monopoly game I saw what I was up against and I had a feeling that the ELEDA was going to work on my behalf. By asking the Self-Existent One my Ghost touched the abode of the ELEDA and because this is the place where visions come from, I got the result and threw eleven on the two dice.

The spirit, like the common cold, doesn't show you the results before you catch it, but it manifests itself while you're going through the process. Whereas with our Ghosts, or you would call him or her, the inner man or woman, there is a landslide difference. The change is this: with the Ghost there is a direct vision between you and ICALABORA, no interferences from your spirit or flesh or any other intermediation. The difference between a vision and a dream is that a dream is a part of our spirit and fleshly build up and a dream can be forgotten about at any given time. A vision, on the other hand, is far more superior in its significance and I would even go as far as to say vivid to our minds.

I think by now you get the message that I call your inner man or woman your Ghost. So for the reader I will gradually, from this point, compromise less while I break it down again.

Before we were robed in the flesh we were created in the Ghost perfect, which is why the spirit can never have eternal life because it has been tainted with corruption. Every man, woman and child's' Ghost that has an element of pure human in them will go back to the Self-Existent One. This earth is, for our Ghost, just a stepping stone back to ICALABORA.

I want to ask you a question: if your flesh dies isn't it punished by death? Now to prove that the Ghost is of a different entity from the spirit, we know that the Ghost within us has never done anything wrong from their creation, so it goes to be with the ELEDA at the abode where boundaries have no end. Yet, and I say yet, the spirit which corrupted its way upon the earth gets the full penalty of the Self-Existent One's anger.

In the next paragraph I will show you a fact but to the reader I will use the words 'reality' or 'fiction', just not to upset the reader and not to compromise at the same time.

Come, I will take you on a journey, whether reality or fiction, come, walk with me. This is the beginning of time as it was for the flesh and humans started to multiply on the face of the earth and our knowledge was vast as far as synchronization goes. If we look back from today at some races we will find that they evolved while others were pure humans, for example from monkey and then through stages to Neanderthal. So in other words part of Darwin's theory was correct, only he missed out the facts that scientists have now filled in, which is that Africans are the only pure humans. While other civilizations were deemed as backward and by pointing out the word other civilizations, we have to take into account that animals too have civilizations. Take the bear, for instance and other animals they would have hierarchy, they live in caves and the ants have nests and like the birds, and so on.

Now when the evolution appeared and the monkeys went through the stages to become Homo erectus and then on to Homo sapiens. Then the Africans, because they were travelers, erected great monuments and helped less fortunate Homo sapiens build their civilizations while interbreeding with them. Let's not get it twisted; if the Africans could build the pyramids that still hold the secrets of time, how easy would it be for them to go global? All this information can be found out in the history museums, the information that I have given you can also be found in Genesis chapter

6/1/7, this is the original reason why the earth was destroyed. According to the bible

You may not know it but if you believe the bible, this is one of the reasons why the earth was destroyed.

It was because the sons of God cohabited with the daughters of men. So the God of the bible got mad and destroyed the earth with the flood.

Now the conquest of Africa initially really started five thousand years ago, when they opened their gates to trade. The Europeans and others, amazed with what they saw, became filled with jealousy. That, my friend, was the beginning of the manufacturing of the spirit.

What I would like you to understand is that the ELEDA never created anything that was evil. That first state of jealousy led to a multitude of fractions of split personalities, among the spirits in the people and that spread like a bug. This my friends is what we call the original virus, and have no doubt about it if something has two genders, I'm talking about the spirit; good and evil, then you too will have to agree with me that the ELEDA, never had no part in its creation. This whether reality or fiction is feasible; Can you question it?

Like the common cold can be caught, it is the same way that a spirit can influence or govern a person's day to day life if they allow it to. If you are honest with yourself and look at history you will find out that the truth is in the eye of him that beholds.

CHAPTER 2

Our cycle of life never ends. First we're created in the Ghostly form by the ELEDA after that we are made and fashioned by the self same Self-Existent One. Please give me time to break it down to you because at this moment I'm going beyond the beyond. Before the Ghost that lays within us left the domains of the ELEDA to be put on this earth because he or she was created perfect in the Ghostly form, so in turn was we made or fashioned in the flesh perfect. As I pointed out to you earlier that the ELEDA never created or made anything evil, would you say that the ELEDA created the atom bomb or the gun?
The ELEDA certainly didn't create those devices of evil and neither did the ELEDA create the spirit that it takes to make these things. That is why, because the flesh became corrupt and the spirit is corrupt, the Self-Existent One will take the Ghosts back to its natural cycle of estate.

I realize that nothing of the combination between the flesh and the spirit is good. Our flesh because it has been corrupted by the spirit, can serve no good purpose but to be condemned and judged by the ELEDA.

I also told you that in the transformation between our Ghost and the flesh our flesh was made perfect. Is it a possibility that this flesh was meant to live forever and the spirit is the reason why humans die? As we come down I will give you the analogy.

So when we die our flesh is destroyed because of corruption and our spirit is judged because there is nothing good in it. Now the Ghost, on the other hand, which was created perfect, takes its abode once again with the ELEDA.

In life there can't be many things we can be sure of and because things are not explained to us, we often dismiss the fact that there is truth in the matter at hand. I'm going to give you an example: somebody says to you that they've seen an alien. No matter how much verbal talk you give them, they will never understand your thought pattern. For instance, if you asked a religious person whether they believe in aliens they will tell you, 'No,' but my answer to that would be, 'It's obvious you believe that your god is a man.'

What I'm trying to say is that you must be in constant communication with your god, then you will give your god no choice but to hand you over to the Self-Existent One.

I want you to imagine this: a man goes to work and he has a bad day at work. Then coming home from work he puts the key in the lock and sits down expecting his dinner. His wife because she has to look after the three children couldn't cook his dinner. He gets angry and stabs her two times. When that man goes to court he tells the judge that he just couldn't control himself.

That is the irrational action of the spirit's demand over what the flesh feels about the whole situation. Now you know that I do extreme because as a scribe it is my job to explain what is happening in the world and the one thing about it is, that we read about it nearly every day in the papers.

The second part to that is the fact that this same man used to bring his wife flowers, everyday for the past twenty-five years without fail. He never raised his voice to his children or his wife and he was so against violence that he would leave the punishment of the children to his wife. That one action of him unleashing the full potential of his spirit will cost him his life behind bars, and not only that but he will always have on his conscience the fact that he's murdered his wife.

I will be the one that tells you that you must, I say must, guard your inner man or woman with diligence, remembering that it is our Ghosts that have the benefits of eternal life. Our Ghosts cannot be tainted with evil but that also doesn't give us the excuse to be presumptuous. Although I preached a gospel that was strange to me, writing this book has just opened my eyes to right and wrong.

If you ever regret the time that you were born, then you in your own mindset will regret the life of your mother, your father, brother, sister, uncle, friends and so on.

I'm talking about suicide. Don't do it; it's not worth it!

Not even murder can compare to suicide because in the act of suicide the person symbolically sees this world as hell and in their mindset, suicide signifies a better place than the position that they find themselves in. My telling you that our Ghosts will be in eternity, with the ELEDA shouldn't make you assume that you're better off committing suicide. Imagine being in eternity with the Self Existent One, showing you the many reasons that you shouldn't have committed suicide. One of the things that I know that the

ELEDA will show you is the effect it had upon your immediate family, not forgetting children and friends.

Suicide will bring repercussions after repercussions and will never rest at one generation. Suicide is the irrational actions of the spirits demands over what the flesh feels about the whole situation.

After years of torment, once you have allowed your Ghost to become free, you will find that the struggle between the spirit and the flesh has no fixation on your Ghost. I would like you to bear in mind that it is the ELEDA that allows certain penetrations from this foreign body. That's right; I'm talking about the spirit because even to the flesh it's a foreign entity.

I now realize that the ELEDA has given our Ghosts the ammunition to succeed in this world, although its final destination is not of this world. We will relive our former life in a more intense way when we reach our abode with the ELEDA.

Let us talk a little bit about unmerited mercy and its true meaning. An atheist doesn't serve the ELEDA yet his Ghost receives eternal life. Unmerited mercy isn't because of, but it is in spite of, all the things we should be doing. How wonderful to know that unmerited mercy is what it is because the ELEDA is the one that provides it. When looking at it from a human perspective there is no logic to unmerited mercy. If you don't deserve something in the eyes of humanity, you should never obtain it.

It's like going for a job interview and everybody else is qualified to do that job. First of all you turn up late and then while in the interview, you yourself realize that you're unqualified to do the job. From the very beginning of the interview everything is stacked against you. Coming late in the first place and then not being qualified for the job. It's nothing that you've done that makes you deserve the job, yet the interview panel chose you. That's unmerited mercy and what I want you to understand is that the kind of unmerited mercy that is exposed to us humans has its effect upon all pure humans.

Walking down the road with my step-son I saw a beautiful rose and I decided to pick it. Well, to my hurt, in the place where I picked the rose there was a thorn that I didn't see at the time. Now we all know that roses' stems are thick, so in order to pick one you will have to apply a lot of pressure. Applying the pressure to the stem of the rose gave me the shock of my life and I screamed out. To my surprise there was a woman behind me and she screamed as well. It's obvious that she could feel my pain because her Ghost was in agreement with my flesh, although being a distance away.

The other example I'm going to show you is how evil the spirit can be. When I had left Jamaica after visiting my parents, within five days after I had left Jamaica and came to England my father died. Then talking to an acquaintance of mine, I told him that my father had just passed away. In his reply to that he said, and I quote, "I'd better water my plants because they're dying." Vindictiveness is one of the many attributes of the spirit and if we look into our own lives we will find out that the spirit knows no better.

On the 30th December 2014 at twenty past nine I went to bed, but just before I went to bed I asked ICALABORA to talk to me. It was at this point the Self-Existent One put me into a deep sleep. After that I had a vision that I was in the same bed but awake. The question that I asked ICALABORA was, "Why were we made?" Notice that I never said 'created' but 'made.' Our Ghost is very specific and intelligent. To be honest with you I thought ICALABORA was never going to answer that question but immediately and without hesitation the reply was, I quote, "You can't appreciate it; even in your Ghostly estate, you could never understand the benefits of eternal life."

What I believe the ELEDA was talking about is the fact that we couldn't experience death, so in our Ghostly estate we had no respect for life eternal; that is why the Self-Existent One made us.

Remember I told you that man has the capability to reason with the Self-Existent One? Well because your Ghost has depths that your spirit and flesh can never attain, your Ghost will ask the most important things in life. What I say is let your Ghost ask the questions, not your flesh because your spirit and flesh can only ask superficial questions of no importance.

There are times when the ELEDA would be dealing with our Ghosts and because of that the spirit in us would at the same time try to discredit us. In these cases you must hold on and neglect not to think that the Self-Existent One is good.

The ELEDA will allow nothing bad to happen to our Ghosts because our Ghosts are the property of the Self same One, although your spirit and your flesh on the other hand, are detrimental to both the ELEDA and our Ghosts.

I'm going to ask you a question and I would like you to be honest to yourself. Its night time and you're travailing in a car and going up the road the wrong way. Would you continue on and hope that no car comes down the other way? Or would you pull over to one side and wait till all the cars are gone and continue? I'm going to give you another two choices. If you could would you in fact pull in at every chance and make your journey to the end of the road? Now you and I know that mistake can only be rectified one way and that is to do a U-turn, even if that means stopping traffic.

Why I gave you this reference is because an acquaintance of mine husband was travailing in his car going down a one way street the right way when a car approached him going the wrong way. They both jumped out of their cars and the other young man stabbed him to death.

I gave you this example because there a multitude of ways and operations of the spirit and flesh but only one way of the Ghost and that's to go the correct way down the one way street of life.

The time is 00:02 and the date is 01/01/2015 by now as the old year goes out with a bang, bang goes the theories of the big bang.

One of the reasons why I spend so much time on the spirit is because I want to make something clear that's not seen as clear.

Your Ghost that lays within you channels its energies between you and the Self-Existent One, constantly searching for the right thing to do. Like in situations where you think it would benefit you to act upon a certain plan. If you're listening to the ELEDA you will obtain the right information.

Is it impossible to know the mind of the ELEDA in a certain situation? If we couldn't it would surprise me, for the ELEDA has the ability to create and also has insight into all that was created and in turn will share with us what is best for us.

We were all round a friend's house; don't ask me why this was beneficial for me to know in the first place but the ELEDA saw fit that I should know and now I'm going to tell you. Round my friend's house there were about six of us and then there was a knock at the door. It was my friend's cousins come down from the country to go to a party at New Cross. His cousins then asked us if we wanted to go; we all declined. On leaving, one of my friend's cousins left something behind and that's what struck me as strange. It's the simple things like this that our Ghosts latch onto and bring to the forefront of our minds. Well the debate on my tongue was: how could he leave from such a distance and forget or not even give the object to someone else? So for three hours I debated on the possibility that something was wrong. On the morning of 18th January1981 there was a knock at my door. It was one of the friends that had gathered round my other friend's house. As soon as I answered the door he said, and I quote, "Guess what." To that I replied such and such is dead. We were so devastated by his death that we never spoke about it again.

Sometimes ICALABORA will, through your Ghost, expose a situation so that you are aware of the possibility of what could happen because for certain I didn't know that my friend's cousin had died, until I gave him my answer to his question. Apparently my friend's cousin had died in a fire. Thirteen died.

At some point in each of our lives the ELEDA will be guiding us, telling us to stop because the way we're going is going to be detrimental, to our outcome with the future relationship that we have with the Self-Existent One. I was stopped by a car crash. Both cars were travelling at sixty miles per hour and the impact was a hundred and twenty miles per hour. In fact that is why a lot of people have been snatched out of this world. Don't get me wrong, it's not because they've done anything bad to die or be killed. I myself can't specify why they have been taken out of this world but we do know that it happens. So they're snatched to be with the ELEDA back into their Ghostly estate.

CHAPTER 3

When we divide the most essential things between the Self-Existent One and our Ghost, you will find that it is in 'ICALABORA'S interest to share with us certain things that we may not be aware of. One way to do this is by divine vision. Many years ago in Jamaica I had a vision and in this vision I found myself walking down the road and in the vision I stumbled upon the first milestone which said: 'Twenty seven miles to go.' Now if you don't understand about milestones, they indicate the amount of miles you have to go to a certain destination. On my journey I came across two more milestones and they both said, twenty-seven miles to go.' You and I know that with milestones the number either decreases or increases, so it did make me perplexed.

On waking up in the morning I told my Auntie and she said, 'Mark the vision.' What she meant by this is, 'Watch for the vision because it will materialize.' Some months passed and I was coming back to England. My mother decided to send money over to my sister to pay for my flight over. I would like you to know that my mother never specified a specific date, for my sister to book the flight; that was left down to my sister. Well, to cut a long story short, my sister booked the flight for the twenty seventh of February. Now I'm going to ask you a question: do you think that's coincidental?

Complicated though it may seem, the ELEDA deals with humans on a level befitting, and I use my words very carefully, for one and all pure humans who are very special in the Self-Existent One's sight.

If we see that we can't strive to make peace let us walk away, and by doing so we will achieve that which we search for.

Our Ghost is made conscious of the knowledge of death and destruction. Knowing this fact; has also humbled the Ghost that lays within us. Although our Ghost that lays within us have eternal life. Just comprehending the fact that the body has to die and the spirit must be judged has given our Ghosts the more reason to line up to that which is expected by the ELEDA.

When our Ghost had their abode with ICALABORA they never knew the meaning of death and could have no feelings on the subject, either good or bad. Although in the transformation the body was made perfect but I repeat, it wasn't made to have eternal life. That domain was strictly created for our Ghost that were created and not made like the flesh.

It wasn't always so with the Ghost, for if at first our Ghost, in the abode where the heavens and the cosmos was formed, knew about death then, they themselves could die.

Now it's time to speak about the ELEDA, the Self-Existent One. Before time was ICALABORA is, for time cannot conceal the fact that the ELEDA existed and still exists. While superior to man, the Self-Existent One's domain is seated way beyond the beyond. Unlike man ICALABORA's presence is that of the omnipresent and again, unlike man he has no feet and hands. Yet if I could just for this once use symbolic speech, I would say that the ELEDA'S feet would be in the deepest part of the ocean and the Self-Existent One's hand would stretch across and beyond this cosmos.

Words have no grasping of the secrets that lays beyond with the ELEDA. I can tell you for a start that man's understanding of the ELEDA'S abode, is very limited because that which seems impossible for man can be fathomed by the Self-Existent One. Our Ghosts alone comprehend a partial fraction of the ELEDA'S existence.

No man born of a woman has the capability of communicating with ICALABORA, except within his or her Ghosts. With head knowledge you can go far. For example, for a politician to become a politician he will have to study politics. The same goes for religion he will have to study theology. Even in sport there are schools of academies. So head knowledge is good as far as it goes but there is a point where you can exhaust head knowledge and then become repetitive. Now when the ELEDA gives you a gift, a gift is different from a talent because a talent is like acquiring head knowledge. Yet with a gift it is a natural substance that is given by the ELEDA and may sometimes lay dormant in the individual's Ghost, until the appointed period where it would best serve for you and the ELEDA.

I will give you yet another example. Being a perfectionist, to write two pages a night a lot of thought is put into my work and to tell the truth, I've never written four pages in one night. That is how compact and informational my work has become. Not only that but because I started out writing poetry, I've learned to cut my paragraphs down to a minimum but still make myself clear.

The creator diagnosed to understand our infirmities has brought us from the realms beyond, to comprehend what it means to be with the ELEDA again. No human being can describe eternal life but our Ghost, has a partial understanding of the matter at hand. What we gather from eternal life is the fact that it is a gift from the ELEDA to the Ghost that lays within us. We obtained this gift when we were being created by the Self-Existent One.

If I should tell you that I'm serving the ELEDA and I'm going to be with the ELEDA then because I've worked for it, it doesn't become a gift but it becomes the result of my service. In serving the ELEDA we can't look at it like, 'What's in it for me?' We have to worship the ELEDA regardless of our situation. When we look at the word 'unmerited' we should put it in the right context because if we break it down we will find out that in religious eyes it only applies to people who are serving their god. So when looking at the truth of the matter in hand, it's because you're serving your god that he's granted you what you would call unmerited mercy.

To worship is to comprehend the fact that nobody has contributed to creation, except the ELEDA who ordained the universe and all that we perceive in it. Only then can we give the Self-Existent One all the honor that is due to his attributes. It is a man and a woman's duty to worship the ELEDA and I add, not praise the Self-Existent One but worship the ELEDA because praise leads to holding another man or woman in high regard.

The fact that we're worshiping the ELEDA with our Ghost and not head knowledge, tells us more than an intelligence that the Self-Existent One is not just a man. Worship is in spite of not having shoes on your feet. In spite of the fact that you want a job and are unemployable, left to wander the streets at night because you haven't got a home; owing the bank money that you can never afford to pay them; losing your job and you've got a family to feed and a mortgage to pay whereas praise is because you have all these things and more.

What is praise? Well praise is because of the many things that have been bestowed upon you. For instance you could find yourself giving praise if you had found a job suitable for you, or the material things you've obtained in your life. Praise is an expression of thanks; in fact everybody gives praise nearly every day of their lives. Whether you give praise to the ELEDA or not it is in a man or woman's build up to give praise for one reason or another. For example a woman has a child. In giving approval for that child, she's also giving thanks, which is praise. A man finds a wife that he is contented with and realizes this is the woman that he wants to spend the rest of his natural life with. Being pleased with his wife he is thankful and in admiration he shows gratitude, so his reaction in that situation is praise and thanks giving.

The ELEDA understands the mindset of the flesh, the spirit and the Ghost. Nothing is out of the reach of the Self-Existent One's grasp. Sometimes we often think, 'Does the ELEDA really hear my cry?' Or when I'm reasoning with the Self-Existent One, how can I be sure that I'm not receiving the answer with my flesh or the spirit? With your flesh you will ask for worldly goods that take up your daily living, while your spirit on the other hand has a completely different in take on things. I'm going to give you yet another example. Take kleptomania. Deep within the person's subconscious they know that they have no need for the goods they choose, yet it is because of the spirit that the person has a compulsive behavior disorder.

If it only affects the poor then you could put it down to the nature of some humans, for if a person is hungry and they have no money there is a probability that they may steal. It's not just confined to the poor though; the rich have their hand in the pie as well.

So with all the barrage of all that is happening, our Ghost has the fundamental by past of all that our spirit and flesh can throw at it. Yet with all the pains and bruises, knocks and so on that our Ghosts receive from both parties the spirit and the flesh, our Ghosts has the ability to shun evil perceptions and have no regrets because of the connection between the ELEDA and our Ghost.

How do we know that the ELEDA is dealing with us on a regular basis? It gives me great pleasure to tell you the difference between head knowledge and the knowledge that comes from our Ghost that have direct communication with the ELEDA. Head knowledge is when somebody imparts the foundation of what it is that you want to learn about, thus making you formulate your own opinions and in some cases it directs your path in life. When the ELEDA is dealing with us it's not like a revolving door situation, where you don't know if you're coming or going but there is a direct structure that keeps your Ghost in tune with the Self-Existent One. Within our Ghost we are made humbled by the fact that one, we are dealing with the Self-Existent One. Two, the ELEDA respects our views and is ready to put in the input that is need for us to keep on hearing the ELEDA'S' voice. This will lead to the constant dealing of the ELEDA with our Ghost and as time materializes we will in fact have a closer relationship.

The reason why I've written this book is because I would like you to comprehend the fact that, even if you say that you've never had an experience with the ELEDA, by me showing you the many examples you would have realized that in reality the smallest function of the Self-Existent One in your life has happened.

Could you imagine being in a world without the ELEDA to guide us? For those of us that have a dependence upon the ELEDA, there is one thing I have to tell you and that's to keep on searching because the same way I found out the name ICALABORA, is the same way that the Self-Existent One will reveal a name to you.

All of us that have read this book will find out that the Ghost that lays within, carries so much importance because it is with this vehicle I'm referring to that we will enter the domains of the ELEDA.

Some people say that there are something's that we're not meant to understand. To that I say, 'Codswallop,' because with our Ghosts it is one of the attributes of the ELEDA to teach us everything and show us to paths beyond the scope of human reasoning.

CHAPTER 4

Most of the things that I will say in this chapter won't surprise you but it will be an eye opener and something to retain while in your daily life.

Each human has the right to know the final destination of their Ghost. We have the right to know that what we're receiving is the right knowledge and for too long now we've been misled. There are certain things that a politician won't tell you or you would never vote for them. Preachers that have studied theology have the choice of doctrine they preach. In fact when a preacher studies theology they study all religions. For instance after they've finished their studies they choose whether they want to become a Seven Day Adventist, Baptist, Anglican, Church Of God in Christ, Pentecostal, Church Of England, Catholic and so on. In doing so the same choice they made for the religion of their choice, they have to comply with what information they can tell their congregation.

We are living in a world where the poor are sick and tired of being lied too. People are seeking religion for comfort when they should be seeking the ELEDA for advice and guidance. It's just like someone that eats for comfort; they can't see that they're putting on weight and that their physical and mental state is being compromised. The poor man and woman are taking drastic measures to make ends meet.

I'm going to give you yet another example. About twenty years ago in the winter season, it was around half past ten o'clock at night, I was just coming from a friend's house in my area at the time. On the way back home I went into a shop and I bought a bag full of groceries. I then stood at the bus stop alone for about five minutes and it was there I decided to leave the shopping right there at the bus stop. I must be honest with you that not all the time I listen to my Ghost, but on this occasion I had no qualms about the matter. Walking away from the shopping and walking about seventy yards down the road, I saw a young man about twenty-four years of age pushing a pram with a baby in the pram. I was all ready to walk past him until he stopped me and asked me if I could give him some money to feed his baby. I didn't take him to the food I just showed him where it would be.

Our Ghosts never seeks for recognition, for the pleasure that our Ghost acknowledges is the approval from the ELEDA. Remember that our Ghosts comprehend the full implications of eternal life.

Our Ghosts serene ability to stay calm; comes from the journey throughout the time of the conceptional creation by ICALABORA. There has never been a time in the existence of our Ghosts when they had an opportunity to beg, ask or plead for something that is detrimental to them. Although the mission in the life of the Ghost is to worship, it's not that alone but it's also to learn from the ELEDA and you and I know that it will take more than eternity to learn the ELEDA'S ways.

After this earth was formed ICALABORA allowed the rain to fall upon it. Well did you realize that ICALABORA can and has counted every drop of rain that has fallen? Each snow flake since the dawn of the earth's time has been recorded, along with the marine life that has died because of man's pollution of the sea. Man has the ability to protect this earth, with all the knowledge they have gained throughout the years. Yet the cutting down of the rainforests is a manifestation of an evil spirit. It is driving away the animals that have their natural habitat among the trees. Marine life is suffering because of man's inability to see the greed they possess over oil. When, in short, man has found out that he can run a car off of water. To run a car off of water an energy generator splits the water molecules to produce hydrogen and this is used to power the car.

All the elements of the earth that man has dug up have destroyed the earth, like iron, steel, oil, gold and diamonds. I believe that they were all put there for a reason. Anything that is hidden is hidden for more reasons than the eye can behold.

Science has improved or stepped up its game in the health department. Yet at the same time the scientists are making germ warfare in their labs to kill off people that they've deemed as unworthy to live.

Now man has decided to pollute the dark side of the moon. This spirit has no boundaries because it works upon the basis 'by any means possible'.

The same way that we look after our children, we should look after this world. If we expect this earth to continue to function in a proper manner, we ought to rectify our mistakes with the ozone layer because for anything that hasn't been looked after there is a consequence. It will suffer and because of the fact that we don't look after it we in turn will suffer.

At the moment we've reached the stage where it's not too late to turn around the situation and become carers and not destroyers. Nature has a way of reacting to the pollution, like hurricanes, whirlwinds, floods and earthquakes. They're all signs of the earth speaking out physically about the damages that humans have subjected it to. Then above all of that man chooses to destroy each other by war. Not to mention the fact that the life expectancy of war-torn countries has exceeded to an all time low.

Did you know that a prophecy can only be brought into action if it is practiced? Now a poor man has no way of bringing a prophecy to reality unless there is an outside influence. I want you to think about what I've just said because in most cases the prophecy that was made was enforced by an outside party because they heard about it. I'm going to be upfront with you and tell you where I'm coming from. Now according to some Muslims nine eleven was prophesied in the Koran. Whether the prophecy was true or not they enforced it so that it became true to them that believed. There is also a prophecy from the Bible that pertains to the mark of the beast. Secretly the western world is trying to implement this prophecy. I say again: whether or not this prophecy is true or not it can be enforced and become a reality.

Understand this, that no prophecy that has anything to do with evil, has any bearing with the ELEDA because his pure and doesn't entertain evil. Either in this life or the next dimension the ELEDA will not tolerate evil.

One message I would like to get over to you is that our flesh wasn't created in the image of the ELEDA because that would be belittling the ELEDA. Our Ghost is the cornerstone of the ELEDA'S likeness though. What am I talking about? Our Ghosts hold a tiny minute amount of attributes that the Self-Existent One has. Like our Ghosts have never been tainted with evil, neither have our Ghosts shared any thoughts of genocide, self harm, jealousy, contrary behavior and the side effects of the spirits inadequacies but with purity our Ghosts strive to be like the ELEDA in more ways than we can imagine.

If ever there was a time that we needed the ELEDA it's now because man's spirit is dominating the world. Out of all the people that are religious, it is a minority that actually listens to their Ghosts. I must tell you that because we are in the flesh, it stops the free flow between our Ghosts and the Self-Existent One.

I'm going to ask you a question: have you ever recognized your inner man or woman and the strength that you possess? Or have you come to terms with the fact that you're holding back on your Ghost? Let me give you an experience that I had with the last book that I wrote. It was so dynamic that sometimes I would leave it for ten years because it was something that was so powerful to me. I'm going to go into the reason why I started this conversation. The book's name is Liberators and it had a lot of facts in it but it was a fiction. Now I know what Salman Rushdie felt like when he wrote his book. I didn't compromise in the book Liberators; I took it to the extreme. I went with my Ghost all the way and after finishing the book I just wanted to die because there was so much truth in the book. I actually told a friend that I just wanted to die out of fear when I finished that book.

To tell the honest truth, I feel more and more humbled in my Ghost for writing this book. Not forgetting the many opportunities that the Self-Existent One has bestowed upon me. The ELEDA has given me the aim of writing this book, which is to share with you my experiences of the Ghost that dwells in me and the ELEDA'S influences. The objective is to show you the connection between our Ghosts and the ELEDA.

Isn't it a wonderful thing to know that our Ghosts will all be at the abode where the ELEDA dwells? That is the security that the Self-Existent One has set for our Ghosts. We can rejoice in the fact that ICALABORA will bring our Ghosts back to its first estate. I can only think of the things that we will do when we get there. For those of us that never went to university and always wanted to go, I believe that it will be a school of in-depth learning and the things that most intrigued us will be taught. Some people study and don't enjoy it but the things that our Ghosts will be learning are the insights into the ELEDA'S domains. For those that were atheist, they will be amazed at the true meaning of unmerited mercy.

I'm going to give you another example. When I was at school the teachers couldn't teach me and being dyslexic made it a harder job for them. I remember being in the fourth year of the seniors and in a special class while reading Ladybird books. Now it wasn't until I had reached the age of about eighteen, when going to jail, that I learned the art of reading. Before then many things had happened to me. Even now I find it hard to read books, to be honest with you I find it easier to write books than to read them.

When I came out of jail I became a preacher of a gospel that I now know as foreign to me. For sixteen-odd years I preached hard according to that gospel. Yet I have no regrets because it was a stepping stone to the things I've learned today.

Taking on board the name 'ICALABORA, the Self-Existent One' isn't easy because people would ask me where I got that name from. All I used to tell them is that it was given to me by the Self-Existent One. I would never explain to them how I received the name in detail. Today I will give you a graphic detailed account of what happened.

I was twenty-one and now I'm fifty-seven so you could imagine how that day stuck out in my head. I was invited to go to church by my next-door neighbor and she could actually see there was a change in me after coming out of jail. When we got to church the message was about Elijah and Elisha. Now the whole message was about Elisha wanting a double portion of Elijah's blessing. All that was in my mind was that I would obtain a double portion of the preacher's blessing. I wanted to take a step closer to the creator because as you and I know, when somebody comes to religion they honestly believe that their search is over. Well I knew that this was just the beginning and what this preacher was delivering was the oil in my cog.

Before I carry on I would like you to understand that my search was ever since I was a little lad. If by now you don't believe that you're special, I'm begging you to ask the creator to show you your calling. Then and only then will you be able to see in the mirror of your eyes the many things that the creator will show you.

Anyway, after the preacher finished the message he gave an altar call. In the church they were well-organized; having special people to deal with those that went to the altar. When looking back now; I can remember in my mind having a big fight about the issue of me going up to the altar. After realizing that I had come to church for a reason, I decided to swallow my pride and go to the altar. What took place next was hard to explain. The ushers started to talk in tongues and it was there that I fell to the floor. They then started to call on the name of their intercessor but when they asked me to repeat the name I would say, 'Us, us, us', and I repeated this until they told me to speak in tongues. When asked to speak in tongues that was the inception of the name ICALABORA. Now ICALABORA'S name lay dormant in me for over sixteen years and now over the last seventeen to nineteen years ICALABORA'S been flourishing in me.

CHAPTER 5

Although there are some people that choose not to serve the ELEDA in this life, that doesn't mean that they have no involvement with the ELEDA in our Ghosts life to come. Strange though it may seem, this book isn't to please your flesh and it surely isn't to justify your spirit. It's to bring common ground between your Ghosts and the Self-Existent One. Unmerited mercy means just that: we don't deserve it.

You might be saying 'What about if the person is evil will they still go to the domain where the ELEDA is?' First of all, it's not the Ghost's fault that the person is evil because as you and I know, the Ghost that lays within you is pure and the one thing about ICALABORA is that ICALABORA has preserved your Ghosts, to be by ICALABORA'S side. If ICALABORA would tolerate the things that the flesh and the spirit get up to, then there would be no need to set aside a place for our Ghosts.

How could I show you the amount of trouble, that ICALABORA has gone through to preserve our Ghosts? I don't think I can but I'm going to try. Can you imagine this? You've been in a coma for the past six weeks. The doctor tells your wife that there's no coming back for you, we will have to switch off the machine because your brain has been too damaged. Your wife then decides to take you home and look after you against the doctor's advice. Year after year passes and it becomes a routine to your wife. Then she herself doesn't believe that there will be any change. Until one day, after ten years your wife notices that you're moving your hand. Because she's so filled with joy she tries to get on to the doctor that dealt with your case, only to find out that he's passed away. That is the amount of patience ICALABORA has with our Ghosts and more.

Religion is a good thing in its purest form but when it's been tainted with doctrine of men it becomes of no effect because how can a book advocate the killing of another human being?

I want you to absorb this in your Ghosts. What's the difference between a killer and a soldier? Well one is a legalized killer and the other is illegal. They both kill the reason why I've written this, is that I'm trying in your mind to eradicate the reasons why we kill. There is no excuse, especially when the murder is premeditated and what other reason can there be but to go to war? It has no part to do with the fundamental fact that our flesh was made. Yet the Self-Existent One perceived this day way back when our Ghost was created, that the ELEDA would have to preserve the Ghosts and destroy the flesh and the spirit because of the destructive nature of the spirit towards the flesh and combined visa versa.

I was speaking to a friend the other day and she was saying, 'What, are we able to do about peer pressure from the government?' At the time I didn't have an adequate answer to give her. Yet now, looking back at the question that she asked me, I can only say because the rich are serving money and the poor are serving gods. The denominator among the rich is one and that is money, whereas with the poor some are religious and some aren't and the divide is a lot. So the poor man not having one voice gives them a disadvantage. Not only that but because religion within itself is, fractional from one belief to another, there is no unity among the poor whether they are atheists or religious. This leaves the rich man to have no respect for the poor because their divided.

After telling her the cause, my answer to the question was that the poor people on a whole, will have to get politically minded in order to fight the corner of the poor. Only a poor man can identify with the struggles of the poor. The rich man will never have sympathy for the poor because he knows that he will have to dig into his own pocket. Can you imagine that 1% of the world's richest people control more wealth, than 99% of the population of the world. It is a fact that the rich are finding ways to make the poor poorer. Now the fact of the matter is that if the poor man ever obtained what the rich man has, he too would entertain a spirit of greed. This spiritual diversity has become like the common cold, once it manifests itself in you it becomes contagious to all those around you.

As for the poor man and woman and this works vice versa with the rich. A man or woman sees that you have your wedding ring on. It's not that they're lusting after you; the spirit is more complex than that. You see, if you know you can obtain a relationship with that person that isn't defined as lusting towards that person, it's defined as two people consenting to a relationship that takes two. Now the complexity of the spirit is this: they don't even want you, they just don't want your partner alone to enjoy the benefits of their husband or wife. What would you call that, what it is? It's spite, bordering onto vindictiveness. Through this book I will break down the many attributes of the Ghost and the template of the irrational behavior of the spirit.

My father once told me that when he was a young man he had meet this young lady and they got to talking but it wasn't until he looked down on her finger that my father realized that she was married. Taking a step back he then apologized, saying, 'Sorry I didn't know that you're married. That was the Ghost in my father that foresaw how the situation would materialize and then took drastic actions to put an end to it.

This is a story of a receptionist that I've had the pleasure of coming across. She only had the one child; doctors said she would never have any more children. The child was then mistaken for someone else and stabbed to death. The receptionist took two years off of work in order just to breathe because she was fighting for her own survival. For a start the devastating fact that she would have to come to terms with a life without her son beside her and also what the doctors told her about not having any more children. After two years of being off work she came back to work with a baby daughter and I've got to mention that she also named the child Destiny.

Thank you ICALABORA, the Self-Existent One, in spite of the fact that her son has gone above and beyond, she will only in this life have conscious visions of him. She will never in this life see him grow old but in the life to come her Ghost will greet him.

Will there ever be peace on this earth? Man has had strife one towards another and in their strife they have forgotten about the ELEDA. People hate people for the colour of their skin but how can this be when all of us bleed? You have something against slim people, why? You don't like overweight people, why? I'm so glad that when our Ghost reaches the abode of the ELEDA he won't be judging us for the things that we've done but we'll be rejoicing in what will materialize as a place that peace dwells. I want you to keep in mind that our Ghosts have been created pure and still are pure.

How can I describe our Ghosts within? It's hard but I'm going to try. When looking into the mirror it doesn't give you the correct image of yourself. How you see yourself isn't how other people see you. The mirror is just a reflection that brings out a similarity because it just isn't you. If everybody's eyes are different, then they can only perceive to the degree they can see. So the invisible state that our Ghost is in now is likened to looking into the mirror and not seeing the reflection of what the mirror would put out but actually seeing you the way people would see you. Now when we reach the abode of the ELEDA, our image will change to accommodate that domain. It's like the transformation from a caterpillar to a butterfly. The butterfly represents the invisible Ghost's butterfly, as it goes through its manifestation when our Ghost has its abode in the ELEDA'S domain. The butterfly is like the inner man or woman. Now when the butterfly is made manifest, which it will be in the abode where the ELEDA has his domain that represents the invisible inner man or woman becoming visible.

Just like the Ghost is the invisible you that was created and also was manifested in the domains of the Self-Existent One, when we return to his abode we will have back that format. Like when you walk away from the mirror and somebody sees you, they see the true image of you and not a reflection, or the consequence of an object that would try to portray the image of the original.

The most exciting joy that one can behold, is the fact that they will be joining ICALABORA in the abode beyond. Our Ghosts are actually in mourning over the fact that they have been separated from the ELEDA'S domain. Just like when a mother is separated from her children, they grieve. Well the ELEDA is justified in saying symbolically that the ELEDA wants all his sons and daughters back. Could you imagine if there was no hope for us whose flesh and spirit have been tainted by corruption because in one way or another we've all made mistakes.

Let us talk a little bit about the desires of the flesh. The flesh seeks to please itself and it will go to any lengths in order to do so. The flesh not only lusts after a woman or a man but it also lusts after things that it cannot obtain. Imagine this: a man has a family with four children and a mortgage. Yet he's always wanted an Aston Martin car like the one that his friend drives. There's no way he can afford it without getting into debt but because of the lust of the flesh, he must obtain this car no matter what the consequences. In this situation the flesh overrides logic and, as I once said, this is the irrational behavior of the flesh's demand over something that isn't feasible. That is just an example to give you the shape of the flesh's demands on things and the unscrupulous irrational actions that the flesh will take.

Now let's look at the spirit and the driving force that allows it to keep on attacking the flesh. I could only imagine that in the beginning the flesh would fight against the spirit but because of the desperate times we are living in it's as if the flesh has given up on its own survival. Why do I say this? Let's look at society from the banker that is corrupt, to the local shopkeeper that charges one pound for something that cost 99p. Now remember the spirit, which is the product of the flesh, can make the flesh be easily influenced by the spirit because the spirit is more potent. In this situation the shopkeeper will say, 'It's just a penny,' and the banker will say, 'I never meant to hurt anybody.'

One goes to the extreme and the other pinches but both of them steal. I lived in the world of extremes and also in the world of pinching.

The question I put to you is: do you think the flesh can live without the spirit? Now the answer to that question is most definitely 'yes' because the flesh started its journey without the spirit. My reference is drawn from people like Buddhist monks, nuns, Christians, Muslims and so forth people of religions that are living according to their Ghosts and not according to the traditions of man. However, our spirit can't live without the flesh because the spirit is a byproduct of the flesh. So when the flesh is condemned by death the spirit is also judged.

Going on to our Ghosts: our Ghosts have no influence over our death, or they would be tainted with our blood. But one thing I can assure you of is the fact that when the body is dead we will ascend to the great abode of the Self-Existent One's domain. ICALABORA preserved our Ghosts because of unmerited mercy to all, those that belong to him. If it was given to a select few then it wouldn't be unmerited mercy. It's like having a group of twenty-four children and pointing out six of them and saying, 'You're coming with me, and we're going to Disney land. 'Is that unmerited mercy? No, from man's point of view it's favoritism. I gave an example about a man going for a job interview against the odds and I also told you that unmerited mercy in the eyes of man isn't logical. Understand this: being lenient isn't unmerited mercy, it's being lenient.

ICALABORA has made it his business not to allow our Ghosts to get too attached to the simplicity of this life and what it holds because the ELEDA'S domain is more attractive than any other possession known to man.

I remember being thirteen and a half and playing round the back of my flat, we had a washing line and a pole made of bendable fiberglass and with that we would play pole vaulting. Although I really liked athletics, I struggled with this game while Barry found it easy. On this particular day, which was the first day that I tried this sport, I had a bad fall and from that fall all I remember is going to bed for the whole weekend. Come Monday I walked to the hospital and on arrival and checking in, the doctor distinctly made a point of asking me how I got there. After telling him that I walked, he then made it clear that I would need an operation immediately. I had punctured my left lung and would have to drain the fluid off of the lung.

This is the many reasons why I want to serve ICALABORA because of a truth that ICALABORA has been good to me. I went from dyslexia to the clutches of death, not forgetting being in prison and then becoming a preacher and after all that, writing three books. With me it's a must that I worship ICALABORA; I have no choice.

When we equate the fact that our Ghost is being dealt with by the ELEDA, for this reason there are measures that our Ghosts will take against our flesh and spirit. For instance rectifying your mistakes although, in the norm they may never have been spotted. You see our Ghosts can have no command over our flesh and spirit if our Ghosts, have little conscious dealings with the Self-Existent One.

There is a difference between consciously dealing with the ELEDA and unconsciously hearing from the ELEDA. The difference is this: when consciously dealing with the ELEDA our Ghost's thoughts are made alive to hearing the things that pertain to the ELEDA and how the Self-Existent One will organize our day-to-day living. On the other hand when our Ghosts aren't connected to ICALABORA, consciously we often find ourselves entangled in the web of the flesh and our spirit. When I speak of unconsciously dealing with ICALABORA, that doesn't mean that you have no dealing at all with ICALABORA, it just simply means that our dealings are unconscious.

How can one define ICALABORA? Well to tell the truth that is the hardest thing to do because even in man's search for peace he stumbles upon deceit, inhumane behavior, lies, corruption and destruction. So for me to define ICALABORA in my little mind I'm going to try. As man; goes in search of beauty ICALABORA is beautiful. When man has the opportunity to look for peace ICALABORA is peaceful. When a man seeks to give someone the highest admiration then that is due unto his title the Self-Existent One. When we consider how far man has fallen, ICALABORA has the unmerited mercy to lift us up through the transportation of our Ghosts.

The vast domain of the ELEDA'S power is the ELEDA'S entity, and that is far above and beyond any comprehension of the human intellect. To compare every human's knowledge that has been born into this world and put it all into one, against the knowledge of the Self-Existent One, then we would still be found wanting. A dolphin goes out to sea and sees a man is left stranded at sea. Noticing that there are sharks around him, the dolphin can think of nothing but to save his life. This is the only creature of the sea that takes pride in saving humans from the sea. That is how much pride the ELEDA takes in providing, a safe haven for humanity by allowing our Ghosts the security of a place of eternity with him.

CHAPTER 6

Beyond dark space where gravity has no significance to some, is the abode of the ELEDA and there my friend, lies the eternal place of our Ghosts' final dwelling. Imagine if light travels at 186,000 miles per second, travelling at the speed of light it would take 8 minutes to get to the sun. Now the sun, is supposed to be 93,000,000 miles away from the earth and it's the nearest star. So could you imagine going to the next star afield?

Now there is no actual proof that the sun is a ball of fire and there isn't a dark side. Not to say that the sun isn't a ball of fire but it has a dark side. I must tell you that in an eclipse, if there was no dark side, then how come when an eclipse happens, this ball of fire doesn't light up the sky from behind? That is because, my friend, there is a dark side to the sun!!!

This is just man's speculation, that the sun is 864,000 miles across and about 109 times diameter to the earth. If man is right then the sun is nearly a million miles across and also if they're correct about the sun being a ball of fire then how come when they take pictures of the sun from outer space you can only see a hallow coming off of the sun? With the sun being 93,000,000 million miles away from the earth, and nearly one million miles across, if it is a ball of fire how come it doesn't light up the dark space for about 30,000,000 miles surrounding itself when they're taking their pictures?

If the sun can shine from the sky 93,000,000 million miles away onto earth and supposedly still be a ball of fire, then why can't it shine 93,000,000 miles into outer space in all directions?!!!

Yet again an eclipse is proof that there is a dark side to the sun, or there would be no such thing as an eclipse. Again, if the moon stands before the sun and the sun can no longer give its light, we are seeing the light side of the moon, which is shining onto the light side of the sun and that should bring more than a hallow.

I would like you to imagine this: you're sitting at your desk to your computer; you have the light bulb on which is a hundred watts, doesn't it light up the whole room and all the space around it?!!! Again you live across the building from somebody and they have no curtains to their house, if they turn on the light in the kitchen the dark space disappears. Just like the sun if it was a ball of fire it should light up more than just the space around it. .

Man goes to space and takes pictures of the sun aren't they nearer to the sun? So why shouldn't they see the sun positioned in the sky as a ball of fire that is giving off its light in all directions???

There is definitely a dark side to the sun the more I think how ICALABORA has given me this knowledge, the more I realize that for too long now we, as humans try to brainwash one another with theories that can't stand the test of time.

This information is from my Ghost to your Ghosts, so weather you believe it or not it doesn't matter because your inner man or woman will capture the true essence, of what my Ghost is telling your Ghosts. Remember I told you that ICALABORA in the depths of his abode will, impart information to our Ghosts on a scale that is unfathomable to the natural mindset. Well to tell the truth that is the comprehending factor of, the Ghosts within us and their ability to gather knowledge from the source, ICALABORA who will not hide knowledge from our Ghosts.

I must have been about five years old, so that would have made it 1965. That was the time I had my first vision, and by the way I've never told anybody this but when I saw the results, of what happened it was more than frightening to gaze at. Again the ELEDA put me in the depths of sleep and there the ELEDA took me to my usual playing ground, which was the local graveyard. We would play things like football, cricket and other games there and when you look to the left of the football ground, you would find a clock tower. Well in the vision it was in the day time. I wasn't scared but I was running for my life. I didn't know what was happening. Trees were falling all around me. Although the experience was frightening, as I said I wasn't scared. At that time I didn't know what a storm was; all I knew is that the elements were out to kill me and if I hadn't been so agile in the vision they would have engulfed me. I was jumping over and skipping between the trees. The more I would try to escape them the more they would be on the attack. Making it to the entrance of the graveyard and being in tack gave me much joy in the vision.

My security was in the fact that I loved the ELEDA, not because of the many benefits that the ELEDA has bestowed upon me, but because the Self-Existent One has my interest at hand. So that was a warning to my Ghost and for that whole week I became weary of the graveyard and didn't go there. When I did finally go to the graveyard after a week, I saw the after effects of the disaster: it was a storm. What I saw did frighten me because there were broken graves and most of the fencing had been removed. It was a cleanup job after a storm. To tell the honest truth, I don't even know when it actually happened in that week but I saw the evidence with my own eyes.

A good friend of mine the other day, told me of how the Ghost was in operation in him. Although he didn't mention the word "Ghost" we both agreed on the term 'inner man', whom I call your Ghost. Anyway, he was originally born in Zimbabwe and in Zimbabwe his trade was a journalist. Misfortunes came upon him and he was out of work. At that time his daughter was about one year old and at this present time she is twenty-one. So let's call it twenty years ago this happened. Before I go on I must tell you that he says that he remembers it like yesterday and that is because it was given to his inner man, or I would call him or her our Ghosts that lays within.

Now, as I said because of misfortune he was out of work, not to his blame and he had a mouth to feed and that was his daughter. A friend of his told him that he should go to Johannesburg with some leather jackets because they were in demand over there and he would get a good price for even one. He had never been to Johannesburg before and had only known one friend who was there. He didn't have the friend's address, plus the reason for him to go to Johannesburg was to start to make some money, so that he could feed his family. Anyway he took a coach to go to Johannesburg and on arrival he chose another coach just out of the blue, or should I say that his Ghost was talking to him. Coming to a fork in the road his inner man told him to get off the coach, the coach continued on straight and he took a left turn, walking not even a hundred yards down the road. He then sees his friend sitting in the passageway of this house.

This is his personal experience with ICALABORA dealing with his Ghost. If the ELEDA created this world and all the universes, then it would be easy for the ELEDA to direct someone's path. I'm sure that all of us have a story to tell but can we recognize the stories? All of our Ghosts are special in the ELEDA'S sight and the Self-Existent One acknowledges us even before we became flesh. That is why the ELEDA has empathy with us and can grant to all his people unmerited mercy to their Ghosts.

Sometimes we question the ELEDA and we have a right to because this is the first sign of reasoning. The same way we question our own actions, is the identical way we should reserve the depths of our deep questions for the Self-Existent One. When I was a lad around the age of five I suffered heavily with bronchitis. Although being a strong lad I had no resistance for bronchitis, so around that time I had an attack and was just recovering. On days like that my father would take me to his place of work. I remember it as clear as day because something significant happened. It was around twelve o'clock all I do actually know is that it was dinner time and I was at work with my dad Joseph Brian Henry. We used to go home where he would cook me dinner. On that particular occasion, as soon as I entered the front door I smelled gas, so I told my father and at first he took no notice. At that time we rented a downstairs flat in our landlady's house. We hadn't even taken off our coat when I repeated to my father that I smelled gas. Automatically my father could tell by my reaction that something was wrong in my Ghost. So my dad ran upstairs and kicked off the door to our landlady's entrance hall and ran to the kitchen. It was there he found the landlady's husband with his head in the oven. My dad saved his life!!!

My father and I never ever talked about that day again ever. People who know you well it is their ghosts that, if they are concerned for you that, you should call just in time because we have no friends like each other's Ghosts. Our Ghosts don't share any of the attributes of the spirit like selfishness, dishonesty, argumentativeness, deceitfulness, boastfulness and conniving. While with the spirit it shows all of these signs and more. Now if you can see the manifestation of the spirit on someone's face, it becomes an action that doesn't mean the spirit is tangible or you can feel it. Remember I said that the spirit is a byproduct of the flesh, so it is the flesh you can feel and it is the flesh that allows the spirit to act upon the behalf of the flesh.

For our Ghosts the fundamental assessment of any one situation is guided by ICALABORA, neither are our Ghosts independent of actions outside of serving ICALABORA. When we talk about obedience of the highest levels, we're talking about our Ghosts' responses that are made towards ICALABORA. The things that I've learnt are the patterns of structures in the life of our Ghosts. When something happens to us we completely forget about it but subconsciously it's is in the back of our minds and the fact is that it could be good or bad. The secrets of the mindset of our Ghosts are given by ICALABORA, in the times when our Ghosts are settled and that, is when the manifestations are made clear.

I was speaking to a friend today and she was explaining how her inner woman had its journey with her. She went on to say that she was "In East Ham in East London and she decided to take a different journey from her usual. Now on taking a different route she saw a friend that she hadn't talked to for twenty years but in the past she got a glimpse of him in passing." First of all she saw nothing strange in that because that can happen. The same week her son had ordered some things off of the internet, nothing strange about that but what she found strange is who delivered it: her friend at the end of the week. Is that coincidental? Well there's more to life than coincidence.

Let's look at it from all angles; first of all she decides to take a different route from her usual route, then she sees a friend that she hasn't really had a good conversation with for twenty years. Her son orders something off of the internet and the fact still appears that she didn't have to be in the house at the time of the delivery. Then her inner woman is reunited with her friend's inner man because something more than luck brought them together. As I said, everybody's got a story to tell and it's for you to identify the many stories. Now if the ELEDA has the omnipotence to create this world, and not only that but the universe, then hasn't the ELEDA, got the power to bring two people's Ghosts together anywhere in the world?

Our Ghosts can elevate us to any level possible according to the scope of human accomplishments. I still suffer heavily from dyslexia, yet it is my Ghost that has the ability to fathom the unfathomable depths of ICALABORA. I'm going to give you an example similar to the one above. An acquaintance of mine invited me to go to a club with her in Finsbury Park, this was all done on the spur of the moment and within the space of two hours I was ready. Performing on the night was live bands and on the night she performed. Now when we were about to leave the club, the young lady that I was with was about to retrieve her coat and standing right there in front of me was a friend that I hadn't seen since the age of seven. I would like you to remember that at that time it was forty-five years I hadn't seen him and I'm now fifty seven. At first he didn't know who I was but the amazing thing about it is that as soon as I mentioned my name he recalled who I was.

That is what I call the pattern of circumstances in the life's performances of our Ghosts. It wasn't like we lived in the same area, he lived in the North of London and I lived in the East. It wasn't by chance that I went to the club in the first place. Direction and destiny brought me there and the result was that, in the natural; I saw somebody that my mind hadn't been on for donkey's years. Further on in the book I will give you more life experiences on reuniting.

CHAPTER 7

The more I consider the wisdom of our Ghosts and their miniature knowledge concerning ICALABORA, I think how 'ICALABORA'S knowledge is vast and unfathomable. What we have to understand is that the depths that our Ghosts have is nothing to what ICALABORA can and will share with us. With all the knowledge that man has learnt throughout the years, it is mostly an addition of the knowledge of 'ICALABORA'S vast omniscient power. When I say 'mostly' I'm talking about the things that are beneficial to man, although anything that can destroy another human being, wasn't made by ICALABORA but it was designed by the spirit. Everything that is taken out of the earth is taken out either to destroy the earth, or to make the earth a better place. Yet for too long scientists are seeking things to destroy this earth because of their malfunctioned spirit.

If it is a possibility that the Self-Existent One exists, then why can't he reveal to us things that are graded from the beyond? The credibility that ICALABORA possesses is the fact that he ICALABORA is omniscient, omnipotent and omnipresent so the ingredients are all there. The word 'utopia' belongs to the ELEDA and that domain because as you know man isn't searching for a perfect world, people that haven't got want and people that have want more.

The difference between the actions of our Ghosts and the attitude of our spirits is the spirits bitterness, can be detected only once it's manifested through the flesh. When I say bitterness I'm talking about things like envy, hate and racism. You see there is no need to be envious of anybody who is just like you. Yet the spirit makes it its business to be envious of other people because this is the nature of the spirit. Now hate is a completely different ball game where you might not even know the person, yet you're so full of hatred towards them that it's eating you up inside. Racism can be a product of society or mismanagement in the family home. All I can say to all these dysfunctional actions of the spirit is that you've got to let it go. Think of yourself as who you are and birds flying by, would you build a nest and put it on your head? Then why would you harbor all these things that can only damage you in the long run.

Did you know that the flesh is found liable for the deeds of the spirit only because the spirit is the byproduct of the flesh? What I mean by this is the flesh shows the manifestation of the spirit. If your anger is beyond reasonable doubt, it is the spirit's way of manifesting your next action. A lot can be said about the flesh and the spirit but not so much about our Ghosts. I'm talking about our inner man or woman being so sensitive in order to be obscured from blame. Our Ghosts have a direct approach and weigh up the pros and cons. I'll give you another example. There was a time when I was going to put some money into an overseas account. Time wasn't on my side so I decided to go to a local branch of the same company. On arriving and going to the counter, I asked the tiller if it was possible that I could make this transaction and she replied, 'You can.' Automatically my inner man told me to retrieve my bank book and ask for a business card. I was told that my money could have been lost in transit because first of all, the address that the tiller had me down under was one of my past addresses from five years ago. Yet she was still trying to tell me that I could do my transaction.

I want to you to open up your imagination and imagine if there was no inner man or woman, with the flesh being corruptible for we know that it's perishable by death. Can you imagine the spirit going to be with ICALABORA with all its faults? For a start it is your spirit that sees people and judges them. Even though your inner man or woman says to you, 'Don't say it,' we sometimes fight to get the words out, backbiting, slandering, vicious and gossiping. We're all guilty of it. It's not that we can't help ourselves; it is simply because our spirits are the byproduct of our flesh. So we gather that with our spirits it sometimes commands the flesh and the flesh is obedient to its beck and call.

Our Ghosts are crying for justice and equality and finding none, yet they find restoration in the fact that their abode is not of this world. How could I describe our Ghosts' journey? Well let me start by saying, focus on this because it's possible, our Ghosts' journey started by the ELEDA creating all of us who are his before this earth was formed, Just like the fact that you didn't choose your parents and your parents didn't choose you. It's not the same way the ELEDA the Self Existent One chose you in creation.

The battle between the Ghost and the flesh already have, a multitude of things going on in the natural, much less the spirits behavioral pattern. Our Ghosts journey is to experience the ELEDA'S divine intervention, between our flesh that can and will die and our spirit that is reprobate. Why do I say reprobate? If the spirit like the Ghost could have eternal life that would also mean, that the flesh could and would survive eternal life. So our Ghosts journey on this earth is a kind of cleanup job and my term cleanup job shouldn't be taken lightly. You see the cleanup job is this, from our individual Ghosts inception into creation, our inner man or woman was created to make the journey back to the creator.

The question that is most prevalently asked is, 'Is there such a thing as an immature Ghost? Definitely not if a child can go to school and learn how to read, then what scope of a difference do you think your Ghost has? I also explained to you earlier, that I was five when I had my first vision. I want you to remember that our Ghosts pre-lived our flesh, so even if a child is born and a child dies the Ghost that dwells in them is mature, due to the fact that their Ghost predates their flesh. Now our journey started with the abode of the Self-Existent One, when we were clothed with our Ghosts by the Self-Existent One.

Do you know that you can love somebody without really knowing the reason why? I was once asked by a reputable preacher, at the Royal Albert Hall on the stage in front of thousands of people, two questions, and "do you believe in God'? To that I replied and said, 'Yes I do.' Then he asked me, 'Do you know him?'To that I said, 'no I don't" I was eight years old when this happened and I remember it like it was yesterday.

Although our Ghosts or inner man or woman love the Self-Existent One with all their being, since they couldn't have a proper response to anything detrimental, our Ghosts couldn't have respect for the Self-Existent One. ICALABORA created our Ghosts and made our flesh solely to get to know the Self-Existent One better. So we aren't put on the earth for a trial, as most people would think, but it's because of our Ghosts that will return to the abode where heights have no limits, or depth has no boundary and where there is no inner circumference.

The Self-Existent One actually means that ICALABORA doesn't need anybody to exist. ICALABORA wasn't made; neither did ICALABORA come from anywhere. ICALABORA was, is and always will be omnipotent, omniscient, omnipresent and unfathomable.

This is just something to think about: a man has a vision and in the vision he's standing near a fireplace. The fireplace, by the way, is nearly as tall as the man. All of a sudden a rat; runs across the shelf of the fireplace then the vision ends. He doesn't tell anybody about the vision but he marks the vision. The next night the man goes to bed but he is woken during the night and he just can't understand why until he removes his pajamas top. To his surprise he finds a mouse in the lapel of his pajamas top, his mind automatically goes back to the fact that there was another person in the vision and that person confessed in the vision. You see the other man was a gas fitter and he was always in and out of houses.

On going to his house of worship, to the night service where twenty-three people gathered, the man is angry with the other person. Let's call the other person Steve. But what he doesn't realize is what's about to materialize. Now what happens next is incredible to the onlookers who don't really understand what's going on. Steve is then seen crying his eyes out and by now everybody knows something is wrong. All of a sudden the man who found the mouse in his pajamas top starts, speaking in unknown tongues directing his anger at Steve. Now that this happened, a family member of the man who's speaking in unknown tongues speaks to the man also in unknown tongues to try to calm him down. So there is dialog going on between two people's Ghosts and Steve is crying on the other side.

The moral of this story is that three people's lives were touched. Steve because he did what the ELEDA allowed him to do. Mark the difference between allowed and made him do you see the ELEDA can allow you to do something to humble you in the long run but and I say again, but never will the ELEDA make you do something that you don't want to do that is detrimental to you and others.

The man that had the vision and then found the mouse in his pajamas top, had learned a valid lesson and that was that he had the power to expose the spirit that dwelled in Steve. Not only that but he had learned the interpretation of his own unknown tongues. Although he couldn't interpret other people's tongues, he would know if they were authentic or not.

The family member learned that the power of the omniscient ELEDA, is and will always be down to the ELEDA because the Self-Existent One is omnipotent in all the dwellings, where the Self-Existent One dwells and far beyond.

Religion in its proper context is a good thing because it's supposed to make you a better person. So when a person is usually drawn to religion there are stages they go through. I would call these stages prep school studies on the Self-Existent One. For if you study the philosophy of men and not our creator you will become a suicide bomber or somebody that doesn't take the ELEDA seriously. Yet our first stage is seeking and mark my words, the only way is through religion. It is easier for us to rectify our mistakes concerning our Ghosts and let our Ghosts lead us into the right place of worship.

Our experiences with the Ghost aren't limited because if you try to remember back as far as you can go, we will find evidence of our Ghosts materializing in and out of our lives. I would like you to recount your steps of your life story and think of anything strange that has happened to you. It might be as simple as getting on a train and missing your stop and then bumping into an old friend.

I'm going to give you a 'for instance' after moving out of East London and moving to Enfield, North London, I decided to become a DJ on a radio station. When working there for a month after going on a tea break one day, I walk past somebody that I hadn't seen in twenty-four years. Then I called her name It was my first girlfriend and at that time she didn't recognize me but after talking to her for a while she recalled who I was. We talked for a while and she told me where she worked and that I should meet her after work the next day. Apparently, she had worked one hundred yards away from where I had worked as a DJ. The next day, after she had finished work, we met up. Now all that happened because she went a different way than she usually goes. That, my friend, is the evidence of the structure of the life of our Ghosts that lays within.

If you're not making waves for yourself, yet you feel comfortable then something's definitely wrong. When I say making waves I'm just talking about you being happy. When did you last go to the pictures alone or with the one you love? Or can you remember the last time that you were filled with so much laughter, that your belly felt like it would explode? Well I'm here to tell you that you can once again, have those times just let go. Let your inner man or woman lead you because that's what he or she is there for, to make you understand your calling and for you to be closer to the ELEDA.

On the eighth of March 2015 at about three o'clock in the day I was on the internet, speaking to somebody that I had only spoken to once before on the internet. Now he used to go to my school but somehow I can't recall meeting him. Anyway he knows my brother really well and because I had left something on my page, in his response he carried on writing about it. So when I had seen his notes on the subject I immediately got in touch with him. This had been the second time I had got in touch with him; the first time was when I had left something on my page. When our discourse had finished he said before finishing, 'Say hello to your brother for me.'

It must have been about one hour or so after that I get a call from my brother. He then tells me that he rang his school friend out of the blue, who he hadn't rung for a long time and his school friend, tells him that he was just speaking to me on the internet. That, my friend, is the demonstration of the persistent telepathy between the lives of our Ghosts.

Every day in our lives something happens but it's for us to be aware of it. I am about to tell you another true story; this happened on 9/3/2015. I was an advocate for a friend of mine that had been diagnosed with schizophrenia. Now she had a C.P.A. meeting which is a Care Plan Approach meeting. In the last two months she's had two C.P.A. meetings because she wanted a change in her medication. The thing was that two people were objecting to her having the change of medication. The two people said that if she didn't take the Risperidone injection she would relapse.

It was my job to support her the best possible way in her favor. The thing about this case is that she wouldn't tell me anything about herself, so in most of the two meetings I would have to depend upon my Ghost to give me the information about her. In the first meeting the doctor talked about how the injection was making her feel, to that she said that the injection was causing an imbalance in her day-to-day living. When it was my turn to speak I said, 'I think we're missing the point.' I would like you to remember the fact that the young lady that I advocated for never gave me the facts on how she came into the system.

Though there was so much opposition to the fact that she should come off of her injections, I knew that I had to let them look at it from a different angle. So in the first meeting I told them to look at the way she came into the mental health system, I suggested that when she was diagnosed with schizoaffective disorder it was the wrong diagnosis. Now I was taking a big risk because I was going up against the mental health field, so I had to prove to them that what I was saying was feasible. Now because she hadn't told me anything, I couldn't tell her what I was going to say. I started off my case by saying, that she was diagnosed with schizoaffective disorder but in fact suffered from postnatal depression. Anyway I proved my point but in the first meeting they still never removed the injection, although they did put in her records that she originally suffered from postnatal depression. This was the first step we had to go through because it was put into her records. After coming out of the meeting, she asked how I knew she suffered from postnatal depression I told her that my Ghost, educates me about things that I could never find out in the natural.

Now that we had gone through the first tire, on 9/3/2015 the second came around. This time it was a male doctor so I had to appeal to his caring side. I presented my case by saying, 'Imagine if she was your daughter and she had been wrongly diagnosed.' Then I went on to the fact that she was given antipsychotic medication when she should have been treated with talking therapy, psychological treatment, cognitive behavioral therapy or antidepressants. The doctor agreed with my concept and wanted to take her off the injection in six months time.

Now the only reason why I can think that this was possible was because my inner man, dealt with her inner woman, on secrets that she wouldn't share with anybody. For this the Self-Existent One deserves to be worshiped because ICALABORA had mercy.

Our spirit's temperament is to destroy everything that ICALABORA has made and created. For a start, it seeks to wipe out the fact that the Self-Existent One exists, by also teaching children in schools that evolution is a process that all humans went through, they are driving a portion of humanity away from ICALABORA. Then by belittling ICALABORA, they've got the audacity to say that man was made in his image. Could you imagine if ICALABORA was in the image of man, because that works both ways, then how could he be the creator?!!

The difficulty in comprehending the Self-Existent One in the flesh is that, the flesh can't get past the fact that ICALABORA isn't a man.

CHAPTER 8

Like educating a child, ICALABORA will educate our Ghosts because it's the duty of ICALABORA that we're well taught. Now the secret of the education of our Ghosts is the fact that, we learn the essential things to edify ICALABORA alone. How can we say that we stand for the ELEDA when we know nothing? We have to be knowledgeable so that we are able to tell everybody who we represent. It is also our Ghosts' duty to search for facts no matter how much truth may hurt, you see truth can damage the credibility of our belief in who you believe in. Rectifying our mistakes is a good thing because it brings us to the beginning of the knowledge concerning ICALABORA.

If there are certain questions that we choose not to ask the ELEDA, then those are the questions that we should be asking the ELEDA. Knowing that our Ghosts are in union with the Self-Existent One, gives us the opportunity to be free to receive revelations from ICALABORA. 'ICALABORA'S unmerited mercy also includes imparting information to our Ghosts and because our Ghosts are pure, they receive untainted knowledge from ICALABORA. As time accumulates and our Ghosts start to hear from ICALABORA on a regular basis, it is there our

Ghosts get to know a miniature part of 'ICALABORA'S will for them.

Once again I repeat that our journey on this earth isn't a test but it's to let our Ghosts recognize the implications of death and eternal life and our Ghosts' response to 'ICALABORA'S unmerited mercy. When I say unmerited mercy I'm talking about everybody's Ghosts, who are sons of ICALABORA, going to be at the abode of the Self-Existent One's domain even though, this flesh is rotten and our spirit is corrupt. Where do I get my information from? Well to tell the truth it's given to my Ghost by ICALABORA.

Deduced from the fact that our Ghosts unlike our flesh and spirit have eternal life and are directed by ICALABORA'S unchanging unmerited mercy, every pure human has been given a chance, now the chance is this: to be revealed to ICALABORA pure and innocent. Can you imagine if none of us had the opportunity to meet ICALABORA? In most religious eyes we only meet the ELEDA for judgment and not for anything else. Yes they do speak about the pleasures of being with the ELEDA, but in most cases they expound on the fact there is a heaven and hell.

The subject that I'm about to go into is a very delicate one because it involves the fact of whether or not the devil exists. Imagine the ELEDA knows everything yet he didn't know the havoc that the devil would bring to this earth. Is it possible that the all knowledgeable ELEDA could make this mistake? By having this thought it would be belittling the ELEDA and all the Self-Existent One stands for. Also take into consideration that the Self-Existent One never created anything evil, and I use the word 'created' not loosely because the devil was supposedly created.

If you believe that the devil exists then all his power is attributed and comes from the ELEDA. The question is why would the ELEDA create the devil if in the beginning the ELEDA knew his behavior pattern? You see if you believe that the devil exists then you can't separate the ELEDA from the devil. If the spirit is a byproduct of the flesh and our Ghosts are created by the Self-Existent One, then what and where does that leave the devil to come from? Could it be that when the Self-Existent One created the devil he was created evil? If you believe that the devil exists, then you believe just as much in the ELEDA as you do in the devil. Once you believe that the devil exists, the self-existent one and the devil become inseparable. As much as you believe in the ELEDA and you say you believe that the devil exists, your belief in the ELEDA is just as equal as your belief in the existence of the devil.

I'm going to ask you a question. In your mind can one exist without the other? And why couldn't it just be the good entity? I believe that the spirit that dwells in the majority of us is that, that has an evil persona and it is that that is the driving force of all evil. For if the ELEDA won't force you to do something that you don't want to do, how can you say that the devil has the capability to tempt somebody when all we ascribe; to the ELEDA is the fact that the ELEDA won't force us to do what we don't want to do?

Here's something else to think about: a watchmaker decides, after twenty-five years in the business, to make his own watch out of all the spare parts that he has. Let's just say for instance it's a quartz watch and to finish the watch it will take him four years. Four years later the watch is up and ready and has been working for the past ten years. One day he wakes up and looks at his watch and his watch's big hand is going backward. First of all he shakes the watch thinking that it's a temporary fault. What he can't figure out is the fact, that it worked for ten years and never gave him this sort of trouble. The watchmaker then pulls the watch apart, knowing there could be nothing wrong with the watch because it worked for ten years. He doesn't know what to do so he gets a friend to look at it for him. His friend tells him that he can't find any fault with the watch. So the watch maker decides once more to take the watch apart and try to fix it. He can't fix it so he scraps it.

The moral of this story is the fact that the watchmaker made the watch, he didn't create it. And furthermore, he didn't know the outcome of the watch unlike the ELEDA that knows everything. In the eyes of the believer that the devil exists, why didn't the ELEDA know that the devil would betray the Self-Existent One? The watchmaker didn't know that the watch would pack up on him because he's not the Self-Existent One.

Let us talk about the real matter at hand, the spirit which symbolizes the devil. But, I repeat but, it is not the devil. Now the devil I have no command to speak of. What I can comment on is something that I know to be true. Now the spirit is of dual personality and doesn't know good from evil. Take a perpetual liar although at times they would seek to tell the truth, it doesn't lie in their spirit to compromise with the nature of the spirit that possesses them. What can I say about serial killers? They want to get caught, but in their own time. They specialize in playing the ELEDA with people's lives. The serial killer's ambition is to carry out the mission of the spirit that inhabits that person. With the adulterer they feel alone even though they have a husband and the spirit just might fulfill their need in a man that is similar to their husband. These three examples are just a few of the behavioral patterns of the spirit. In most cases they apply on a whole to many operations of the spirit.

My mother once told me a story about what had happened to her. I would like you to bear in mind that my mother died at the ripe age of ninety-two. She told me that when she was a young girl, she had an experience with the ELEDA. By the way, just so that you will feel a little of the experience I'm going to mention her name. There was no food to eat but Belzie got sticks together and stones to build a fire. Belzie was too young to even conceive of the fact that she could be hungry in Jamaica. So Belzie put the pot on the fire that she had. Belzie then went to the nearest bread fruit tree. Now if you don't know what bread fruit is, it's nearly as big as a volley ball and it has a green outside and a white inside. I would like you to remember that the pot is on and the water is in the pot. Saying that, when a bread fruit is ripe it drops off of the tree and the one that drops off of the tree is roasting breadfruit. But some breadfruit can stay on the tree and still be roasting breadfruit and the one that you pick from the tree is boiling breadfruit.

Now Belzie, from a tender age, had learned to trust in the ELEDA because in Jamaica in those days that's all you could do. So Belzie goes under this bread fruit tree and raises her hands as if she's willing the bread fruit to fall into her hands because she knows that with the ELEDA it is possible. The fact that I would like you to take into consideration is that it was a boiling breadfruit and wasn't ready to fall off of the tree yet. Although, through the unmerited unchangeable description of the ELEDA, my mother was able to eat, the bread fruit that had been waiting since eternity. It was made possible that my mother could do a simple thing like eat thanks to ICALABORA.

Thank you, after the many things that you've done for us how could I not thank you?

When I was seventeen I got myself, once again involved with the law. Now on this occasion I was sent to Borstal and just before leaving they would send you on home leave. While on home leave for people that had been in captivity in that area, they had a project going and they would film the outcome of the project. One of the things that we did was that, one of us played the judge and another defendant. Now four people were given sentences to give to the defendant. Each of us was given different sentences to give him but none of us knew one another's sentence. I would also like to tell you that up to this day I don't know what the other sentences were. So we all had to present our case and all of our cases were presented in a different way. I noticed that everybody else spoke as if this was the first hearing, but when it was my turn to speak I came with the angle that he had been on remand in custody. Anyway, on my card the sentence said 'three months'. So in order to get the three months, I would have to show how he was misbehaving while on remand. Not only that but in order to get the three months I would have to convince the judge to give him nine months. So I started my discourse by saying, he's on remand yet he's showing signs of aggressive behavior. When walking through different wings, and seeing the other inmates cleaning he would leave scuff marks all over their floor. To the prison officers he'd show no respect. If we don't give him nine months he's bound to reoffend.' Just as I thought, he got three months.

This is what you would call synchronization from the time gage, of the Self-Existent One given to our Ghosts that lays within. It wasn't the amount of words it was the substance of words and the angle that ICALABORA took me down.

Man says that the sun is 93,000,000 miles away, can you fathom that? Can you really fathom that?

If this earth did come out of an explosion wouldn't it be in chaos? Why do we see the moon at night and it's not in place of the sun that brings in the breaking of the day? If everything never had an order designed by ICALABORA we, my friend, would have eight legs like a spider. The human that believes that ICALABORA is a man is apt to fail, for he would have no degree of understanding concerning omniscient or omnipotent. Let us just say that the ELEDA doesn't exist. How can you explain the fact that the sun is supposedly 93,000,000 miles away? I hope you know where I'm coming from. Can you see the precision of ICALABORA that ICALABORA set the sun 93,000,000 miles away and not 92,000,000 miles? We're not talking third degree burns; we're talking about over proof scorching point!

That was just one angle; imagine if I were to talk about the trees where oxygen comes from. How do we explain the fact that trees are one of the most important life forces in existence? First ICALABORA, and then comes our Ghosts, after that comes trees. I know that this may seem a bit harsh but not even our flesh is as important as trees because trees support all life forms. The flesh shall one day perish because it's corrupt and shall feel the consequences of the ELEDA. Yet it is said that there are trees that exist that are over four thousand years old. Everything that exists except ICALABORA and our Ghosts has its dependence upon trees which ICALABORA made, can you fathom that? Can you really fathom that? The dinosaurs existed through the life force of trees, if they ever did exist. Not to say they didn't exist, but I have no comment on that.

When we look at the many experiences that I've been through, you will find that you too have been through just as many, but you've never measured them or collectively counted them.

Our divine ability to receive from ICALABORA through our Ghosts, has brought our Ghosts to a greater understanding of 'ICALABORA'S unmerited mercy. Some will say, 'But that person doesn't deserve to be with the ELEDA.' I would like you to understand that it is with the flesh and the spirit that you impute, while the inner man or woman is innocent and always has been. So unmerited mercy is granted to the inner man or woman on the grounds and I say; on this specific grounds that it hasn't been tainted with evil. How can we quantify what unmerited mercy is? Well to start to understand what unmerited mercy is, we have to go to the giver of unmerited mercy whom is ICALABORA. That is why in the first place our Ghosts were created, so that we would stand a chance from our inception. Unmerited mercy isn't because of how you are but it's because of the ELEDA'S gift to our Ghosts. Unmerited mercy can't be supplied by man or woman because they expect something back, whether it's for you to change your ways or an exchange. Don't you think that when our flesh was made that ICALABORA, knew that our flesh would join with our spirit to be deceitful, vain, opposite to all that

ICALABORA stands for, greedy and of an offensive to nature.

Man and woman's greatest fear is death but it shouldn't be because it is there that our Ghosts and ICALABORA will meet. Can you imagine if there was no after life how short our existence would be? Our inner man or woman will tell us the true story of how we ought to live one towards another in peace. I'm going to ask you a question. Do you believe that this world will ever have peace? Let me answer that question, if through religion we can't have unity, then how can we abide under the ELEDA when we're divided in giving thanks; to the Self-Existent One. Man and woman through the flesh and the spirit, have put the ELEDA on a back burner and have set up man on a pedestal. The politicians aren't really seeking peace because war is the way they get paid. They have no regard for life, just in the fact that their bank balance is growing. I would like to think that this world could have peace but none are setting the standard. The only time we will obtain peace is when our Ghosts are reunited with the ELEDA.

Each tear that we cry is engraved on the template of the ELEDA'S heart symbolically speaking, so in all our trails neglect not to think that the ELEDA will and is watching over us. The main objective of this book was to introduce to you a different way of how to look at your inner man or woman whom I call our Ghosts. I think that I've proved, with reasoning, that our Ghosts are recognized as our inner man or woman and our spirit is of a different entity from our Ghosts. I think by now you and I realize that I have exhausted the subject on our Ghosts, the flesh, and the spirit. So I find that this would be an appropriate time to leave the book open, with no sudden breakdown but just to leave the book open for you to scrutinize at your will.

My final words to you is keep on pursuing happiness in the right program and never give up upon understanding things that materialize.

Dermoth Alexander Henry - The Scribe

POETRY FROM A BLACK MAN'S PERSPECTIVE

POETRY
FROM A BLACK
MAN'S PERSPECTIVE

DERMOTH ALEXANDER HENRY

AUSTIN MACAULEY PUBLISHERS™
LONDON · CAMBRIDGE · NEW YORK · SHARJAH

AFRICA

A place to behold with the natural eye
Watching nature develop, in a country that size
As I cover my eyes from the morning sun
And see the fetus, of the land where civilization began.

Rapped in the glory of Pharaoh's and kings
Found to be beyond, the world of architectural dreams
The people disguised, as an ocean of water
Subsequently designed from a GODLY order

How precious the minerals, of my people are
For it's the land of my ancestors, the children of AMEN-RA
Comforted by the sound of the drums, in the back ground as they drop
Hearing the lion roar, and the elephants bellow when they trot

Let me take you on a journey, of a land so unique
AFRICA: the pinnacle of where my ancestors, put their feet
A joy to comprehend, that our history is so deep
As I say a prayer for my ancestors
Who wouldn't take defeat.

Egyptian Dynasty

Although in Africa, Egypt wasn't the first kingdom
Yet it has the most abundant contribution, of dates in a lump sum
To explain the Pharaoh's and queens of Egypt in Dynasty
Is simple
It is a line of hereditary rulers or leaders, of any powerful family

To get more acquainted with Dynasty's
I'll give you a quick analogy
Let us say that you were a king or queen
And you were the first to rule, and fulfill your dream

Then your sons and great, great grandsons ruled
While for them, time wasn't so cruel
So your family Dynasty lasted two hundred year's
From your first rule, to your great, great grandson fall

That explains the rule of a Dynasty
From them that ruled hereditary
Generations of a family

They were versed in the arts
Of astrology chemistry
Even human biology
Mathematics and the structure of science
And even building architectural dreams

Beautiful

**FACIAL IDENTITY
EXPOSESS DELICACIES WITHIN
NATURE'S WAY OF REPELLENTS
BEAUTIFUL**

This poem describes a woman

Beautiful

BODYWORK
STRENGTH OF OXEN'S
RIDES LIKE A DREAM BEAUTIFUL

This poem describes a beautiful car, with a perfect body work and that drives like the wind, an also has the strength of oxen s

Black Icons

When a movie starts, and you see a black actor appear
Don't you just jump for joy and your mind punch the air?
The intense joy, of seeing Samuel L Jackson perform
After so many years hasn't he done well, didn't he reform?

What about Witney Huston, in bodyguard
Wasn't she a star?
Check out Forest Witticker and the emotions in his face
Shows he has complete control of his where a bouts and place

And when Eddie Murphy came on the scene
To us youths he was like a dream
As Denzel Washington finds his groove
If you study him carefully, you'll find he has many moves

I admire the Black actor that doesn't play a compromising roll
Just for a billfold
I believe that T.V shows the reality of rich Black men in America

But more often than not, it describes the depths of the other side

So let's rejoice in people like Blair Underwood, Angela Bassett,
Spike Lee, Morgan Freeman, Queen Latifah or Wesley Snipes,
This for me is just a few of the Icons to mention
But the choice is yours choose one

We've come a long way, from the lands of the Pharaoh' Kings and Queen's
To slavery then to the best actors in the world
Hasn't the Creator blessed us with a voice?
So let's use it.

Blue Beautiful Sky

Beautiful day ahead
Light sunshine rays
Unique flower beds
Eye dazzling birds

Butter cups blooming
Erased is winter
A moment's peace
Unity among animals

The storms over
Irreversible moments today
Full moon tonight
Ultimate transformation ahead
Lovely blue skies

Seventy degrees fathom height
Kindling heat wave
Year's hottest day

Ebony History

Extracted from the pages of a history book
While I tempt you my brother, to take a good look
Shackled in chains and a history denied
Being the first to exist, we still survived

Great empires were built, before the slave trade
On the walls, visions of the past engraved
Testimonies of Pharaoh's hued out in stone
Africa; being the cradle of civilization, stood alone

Man to this day, can't comprehend just how advanced they were
For the concept of a race of people, whose knowledge was pure
Gave them an inferiority complex,
And that my friend, made them vex

Beyond human reasoning, they plundered and raped
And the Egyptians you see now,
Even they know their fake.
Disregard all you've been taught, in schools
Black peoples history, didn't start with the slave tool
What is the solution to the perfect plan?
The Africans hands must go hand in hand
To defend our country the mother land

Fastest Man Alive

Usain lightning Bolt
World's fastest man
Of speeds untouchable

Jamaican by nationality
Hundred meters sprinter
Speed so incredible
Equivalences of cheater's

Rugged style manipulated
Last to start
First to finish

Justifiably the greatest
Running for freedom
Poverty to riches
Life to living

Sea of motion
Speed; tidal diagnosis
Hsain lightning Bolt

Footballs My Game

Through distress, doubt and pain,
I always love Arsenal again and again.
Which team do you know that went a whole season without losing a game?
Arsenal not Manchester United Chelsea or even Tottenham being exposed to football all my life has given me a reason to strive.

I'm just waiting for a scout to recognize me
Because I'm a team player and I ain't greedy.
Playing for a team, gives me something to do
As one day you'll see me doing it for you.
Remember my name KHALIL:

K for keen to play
H for hidden talent
A for anticipating player's moves
L for Lampard, watch out
I for influencing my team
L for loving football

D.O.B 06/07/99

From A Seed To A Rose

Touched by the emotions that moves through my body,
For a queen so beautiful as dark as ebony.
A fate such as this I never ever miss,
As the sails need the wind, I need her kiss.

A frequent reminder of how passionate you are,
My desire goes beyond the moon the sun and the stars.
You're an intellectual of such a high degree,
I'm fascinated by your composure and sense of ability.
Flavored with sugar, your heart shows compassion,

I'll love you forever, I made my decision.
From the intricate parts of my mind so deep,
Your body so perfect, your nature so sweet.

My concept of you is like a rose in bloom,
That's why we've been together, for a million high noon's.
Consistent to you my love for you grows,
Originally from a seed, to a petal, to a rose.

Happy Valentine's Day

As an Oyster encases around its precious pearl
Let my heart be intrigued by you opening to me, your love
in this world
Your beauty is that of the rainbow after the storm
Just as your heart is as precious as a rose without thorns

Contained in my mind is an immaculate journey
Where I take care of you as my queen and priceless special
lady
For you have a quality, that is to be admired by the natural
eye
That; simple depth can't describe your intelligence, but I'm
going to try

When matter was formed; by the Creators hands
You were made to be understood and also to understand
That artistic wealth dwells within your heart,
You're a diamond you're a pearl, you're one special girl

Happy Valentine's Day
xxxx

Kill

Gangs at war
Many games played
Death amongst youths

Honesty among thief's
Jail is eminent
Attitude demands leadership
Aggression paves way

Conscious minds deluded
Best friend; guns
Fragmented family life

Distracted school days
Fend alone soldiers
Qualified for nothing
Lonely road ahead

What quantifies role models?
Morally understanding youths
Best possible output

Kill; bad ideas
Damage; violent thoughts
Hurt; negative action
Slaughter; dirty conspiracies

Love Has

Diagnosed to love you forever
For this fate I know, I will endeavor
As change will come, my mind will think cleaver
While I contemplating loving you, in all kinds of weather

Controlling thoughts brings back different memories
How the mind generates a selection of energies
While it's conducive to dimensional entities.

Love has statistically been good to me
So why shouldn't I be, to them that love me!
Can a lion change its Diet to grass?
Or a cow, change its diet to meat?
Won't it "be consumed by the very thing it eats?

Man How I Love You

If ever there was a man that I adore
Then you my darling are that man for sure
Neglect not to think, that I would ever leave you
For you're the man of my dreams and even my boo

Since I was made for you and heaven was made for angels
You're my man and you were made for my crown jewels
When I'm cuddled up in your arms and I look into your eyes
The first thing that comes to mind, is wisdom and how you're wise

I've never considered my life without you
For you have given me all the inspiration,
I need for true
You've never put me down, or made me feel like a clown
So I'll always stick around

While the heavens unfold and the stars fall from above
Whenever we're together, you can tell we're in love
And as love orchestrates a turning point in our life
It's a joy for me to know, that I'm your wife
Pastor's wife

Many Words

You say you're a politician,
But all you do is cause division.
Then you say we're in search of peace
Yet you break every contract, and it's there your bombs you release.

While in your speech you talk of equality,
Yet on the streets of London,
people are homeless and are dying from poverty.
You talk about starvation as if it's a disease,
Please, please you're a politician,
We're begging you please.

The bible says that all governments were set up by god,
Certainly not my god, but his god,
For HIM whom I believe in, created all things, my
Creator established the seas the heavens and the dry lands
Out of that man made bombs,
Guns and germ warfare by his own hands

Corruption is seeping through the seams of this society,
From the local shopkeeper who charges one pound, for something that cost 99 pee,
To the banker, who gives himself a three million pound raise and justifies it by saying; see

Mr. Robin Walker

A man of integrity and precision
Seven years of strict dedication
To write a book of such range
About the historical history, of the black man's age

As Mr. Walker integrates
A vast degree of intelligence
And adds to our history a knowledge of science
We hope that the communities all over the globe
Will show him due benevolence

Every page is worth reading again and again
Until the information, seeps into your sinus and brains
It's so mind-boggling to know, that this book is so factual
While time is so important, without this book you have no tool

One songwriter said
Who took the crook out of the book?
In his reply he said
It was the crook that took a look

Dry wood will start a fire
While wet beams
Will raise smoke higher

The Book is called
When We Ruled
By
Robin Walker

©1/2/2007

Music

When music is played in the night
It's much different from the day light
It has a kind of surreal feeling
Although at night, it becomes very revealing
The words seem to change to suit how you need healing

Music taps into the soul
And in most cases reveals how one is old
If I say Randy Crawford, one would say early eighties
There again going even further back,
Al Green early seventies
Before them was Brook Benton, an artist of renowned character
Stevie Wonder sixties
Aretha Franklin late sixties
Sam Cook early sixties

Their music reached boundaries that can only be described as phenomenal
Whereas the music these days, I would go as far as to say is sending our youths mental
What can we do to repair the damage that has already been done?
Look around you, our youths killing each other like it's fun

When will our artist send positive messages once again?
Teaching our youths to stay out of trouble and from killing, refrain
I am not here to hinder an artist in his individual belief
But when will they let up and give our children relief

My Father

When I define my location, I find it hard to mention,
As if the time I've taken up is smaller than a fraction
But I know I've made an impression or given advice with great precision,
My eyes conscious of my mind so deep
With the flirtation of thought, that my father will soon sleep,
At ninety-one years his lived so many
For my thirty-nine years, I haven't lived any

As my mind rest upon that final day,
When my father shall surely be taken away,
Let me write, as my pen will give me gravity
For I know that one thing it will not deny me.
Obliged to be his favorite son,
Gives me all the more confidence to know that I'm his number one.
For years I've been anticipating my reaction,
But I will never understand, until reality is my action.

My father, he will sleep the sleep of death,
Yet in my mind, he will be alive in an unconscious rest,
Completely oblivious my reasons has foundations,
For out of every people, people are dying from every nation,
Although my grief is premature, in order to comprehend it,
I will have to take steps
To be more mature

My History

How can you say, my history's gone away
When you can see it's in the walls of Zimbabwe. There's
modified versions, of you carrying baby's on your back
It's just the way that we do it, as blacks

While with modern culture, where everybody wants a tan
But know body wants to be a black man
In R & B they want to dress, sing and even rap like me
It seems like they have mimicked us, all through history

Yet no credit is given to the black man
His history to understand
You've waged war against our children
For deep fractions go hand in hand?

The legacy of slavery, has brought Africa to its knees
And they will continue to do that until, the deficit they freeze.
As far as my eyes can see, the situation will never abate
Until Africa is full, of those who are awake?
From their slumber from sleep, a new nation we need
Too counter-act upon those that have brought us to our knees

©25/6/07

New Found Love

As she smothered me with love
I thought; this is heavenly, this must be from above.
The dynamics was there, every motion of her hand,
As her pleasure took me to the promise land

Exotic tails I once heard,
Now I'm getting it feeling for feeling and word for word.
While I grasp the sensation of these feelings,
They give of a new dimensional meaning.

It was killing me, I didn't know whether to laugh or cry,
The joy was so intense, I started to turn fool and sing a lullaby.
Then her words stroked my intellect,
She said "To forget you is never to remember you,
And to remember you is never to forget you,
I'll always remember you"

She was delicate in every way, as on the four poster bed we lay,
After silence, we promised in life that we had nowhere going, we would just stay.
Face to face as we watched the night passing by,
She said "I love you"
I said I love you to
She said why, "do you love me"

And I said because you're you
Then she said I love you because you're faithful and courageous,
Then to my surprise she said "Swear to god you'll never leave me"
And I said I swear to God I'll never leave you,
All of a sudden she said wear to God you'll never hurt me?
I was faced with a question that still haunts me,
I swear to God I'll never hurt you

I was twelve
She was thirteen

Oxygen

As I bend with the wind,
I've seen many a things,
Being two hundred and fifty years old,
I realize life for you, life is so cold.
What has become of you?
The cows live peaceful,
The cats and dogs too,
You were the last creature created,
Yet among us you're the most hated.
Young men sexually confused,
Little children raped and abused,
Drug related crimes,
Death and murders time after time.
I've seen people hanging from my limbs,
For no other reason
But the colour of their skins.
You know what?
I am just a tree,
Telling you what I see.

Pictures Taken

Depths that can scarcely be known.
As I reach out to a hand, that I've hardly know
Yet time will tell, weather we'll ever connect
Or will this be a journey, just to forget

In this fragile life, faith is the subject that I plead
As I find a common ground or deed
While I define my daily mission
To bring back peace in my life, and every situation

Having thought about my position
Loving another woman, is my ambition
But I seem to always get it wrong
Yet in capturing the girl of my dreams, I'll have to be strong

Just challenge me to make my move
Then I'll show you that my name, comes under the word smooth
Gifted with the eloquence of words
I will speak to you things that you've never heard

Unity

How in the seventies we cared for each other
Not bothering with Ishim's and ski-shims, just love for our brothers
Devising plans that would work together
Having respect and perfect love for one another

Now brothers killing brothers, sisters cheating on brothers
Brothers and sisters, loving each other according to the tones of their skins
Who in our society will win?
Certainly not him that has a heart of tin

A different time spent, it isn't the Caucasian
But our own Ebony people giving us tribulation
The only time we come together, is at funerals
It seems that were not facing up to realities call

We are the most beneficial consumers in the economic market
While providing food to feed the world,
They given us a second class jacket
The Asians are providing food that comes from our country, to feed us
Yet if you was hungry and asked them for a crust
They would send you under a bus

Don't send a car home, send the machinery that can build it
If black people all over the world, would give just one pound
We could sought our financial problem, just one pound weekly
And there we would see clearly.

Unique

She's undeniably beautiful.
A crown Jewell.
Must obtained diamond.

Versatile in style.
Alone with quality.
Subsequently divine creature.
Of quantity's undefined.

Opposed by none.
One in millions.
Benefactor of gifts.

Her love unfathomable.
Delectably arrayed charms.
Eyes like stars.
Number one choice.

Prisoned

She locked me up, yet gave me love
A prisoner was I, like the stars in the sky
Only loosed to be thrown down and die

When will I see life on the streets?
Being locked up just ain't sweet
Can't you see it's stifling in here?
Don't you think I'd rather be out there?

What will I be when I grow old and Gray
Then again, will I ever live to get old and Gray?
Or just stay in jail and have nothing to say

I want to trace my steps, were did I go wrong
Is it my fault that I was so strong?
To tell the truth, I'm a child waiting to be born
Just to come out of prison, just to come out of my mother's womb

Reflection

As I contemplate this journey
I can only say how, things seem to me.
While I reflect, on the way my life supposed to be
What you give is what you get and what you get is what you see

When I borrow from what I've reflected
I know in this life I will never be rejected
If; as an example I sow a good will of seed
What you give is what you get and what you get IS what you see

When I borrow from what I've reflected
Then as a reflection, I look in the mirror
I know in this life I will never be rejected
In this life, I will never reject my achievements
What you give is what you get and what you get is what you see

If as an example, I sow a good will of seed.
And if I keep working hard for what I want to achieve
What you give is what you get and what you get is what you see
In life, if you're doing it well there is nothing called trying too hard. Although some of us fail to understand that everybody is unique, that also = unique individual best. So everybody has their own capability to shine in their own way, and not everybody can shine in the same way. When you see someone trying their best don't judge them just encourage them.

School Days

If I had only known, when I went to school
To listen to the teacher
And not to a fool
I'd be successful now and not re-educating myself in school

Although most things that they taught, were irrelevant to life
I'd have probably settled down, have two children and a wife
When I went to school I was very academical
But they pushed me into sports, and my brain became a wasted chemical

Yet I will not regret the day I was born
For in life, I will race to the tape, until it's torn
Now I m doing the work of a thirteen year old
But I know with life's experience, I won't fold

My dreams are before me, like when I was a youth
But now that I have a record, let me tell you the truth
I've seen beyond my dreams, an just how they've schemed
And I'm going to find my potential, in the blue prints of my dreams

The Journey; Of Karnell

As I capitalize on the idea of success,
I know in life, I will do my best.
For to me, to be poor,
Is to want more,
But to succeed
Is to have, heavens blessed deeds.

You will find I'm talented beyond belief,
While to know my family loves me,
Is a relief
With the voice of cut diamonds, I could find my success,
And my designing skills, that would put a dress on any princess.

For a boy of thirteen; that's my age,
I'll set for all to follow; the stage
Those of you; who haven't heard my name,
It's KARNELL; and life ain't a game.

The Pages Of A Book
Page 131

Come: and go back in time with me
For I will satisfy all your curiosities.
This is for those of you, who really didn't know.
Skeletons of pre-human remains were found, dated
5million years ago

While enjoying your history
Here are your Ancestries
In Omo Ethiopia, human remains were found
Dated 195.000 years old, isn't that profound.

Homo sapiens remains, excavated in Asia were dated at
95.000 years old,
Proving that migration is a possibility as I hope to unfold.
In Africa: it's predominately evident that humanity originated
And from there, all civilizations were initiated.

The oldest human remains found in Europe were dated at
39.000 years old,
While in Africa they engaged in mining 43.000 years for
bronze or gold,

How can we fathom a history so deep?
So perfect in nature

So perfect in speech
It's written on the walls
It's hued out in stone
The mummified bodies:
Yet in all this, Africa's history has now been told
FROM THE BOOK WHEN WE RULED
By ROBIN WALKER

©21212007

The Stages Of Crime

How my friend, can you justify killing a brother
In classification, you're no better than your slave master
By you following others you're driving us to disaster
And not creating any room to Man-oeuvre

As a race that was shackled down to its past
We need to look beyond the slave syndrome,
And see how our historical past continues to last.

Stone buildings in Zimbabwe erected without mortar
Over 1.500 years ago, coins were minted in east Africa
Ethiopia

The Sphinx of 5.000 BC is prove of African civilization
And that our heritage was not just spread over one
destination
But that we Africans opened the flood gates of origin
And set the pulse of all beginnings

Show an interest in your history
Then you'll know where you've been
Where you're going
And where you'll be

To deny such a complex understanding of yourself
Is to deny yourself, the common right to your own health

This Is Poetry

Poetical emotional words
It breaks boundaries
Delightful equational thoughts

Rhyming sophisticated sounds
Mixed emotional feelings
The hearts expression
Meaningful minimized words

Normality's realms broken
The depth unfathomable
Spoken from secrets

Hidden verses tapped
Fourth dimension expressed
Version unto version
This is poetry
This is poetry
This is poetry

Yes its poetry.

Till Time Has Lost Its Span

When captivated by your smile,
That's one of the reasons why I love your style:
As I look into your eyes to me you symbolize purity,
Not forgetting the fact that your life represents such beauty.
It's not hard to write about you,
Because you inspire me to write the things I do.

Go easy on my mind,
For this time I will write as time elapses every line.
Apparent though it may not seem,
You give me aspirations for my long lost dreams.
Even with soft conversation,
Your word becomes a sensation.
Divine to me your voice so free,
What a choice I've made,
Loving you as much as I love me.

What a quantity I share as your voice is open to my ear,
When you speak you speak of life and not despair. In your normal conversations you reach dimensions
That touches my very emotions,
Yet when spoken there is a hidden secret of devotion.
Things that I notice that are true,
You have thoughts for me and I have feelings for you.
Still though I'm willing to wait until time has lost its span,
For my reason for loving you is out of my hands, But I'm a man,
And my birth sign is Taurus so please understand.

Time

Deep in the crevasses of my mind
Select if you will a calling so divine
For if time could manipulate segments
Then time could also justify judgment

How one could observe, one fraction of a word
And not compile the facts, how long is a cord?
From end to end my friend,
Measure it from the start to the end.

Benefits of the blessed are a beauty to behold,
While constructive criticism can make the unsure feel bold
Can a man be starved of Oxygen, and live?
Yet every day we talk boogaloo, while our brains give

What manner of word would I care to speak
Give me a chance and I'll make you feel weak
If I hadn't been born, where would I be?
Certainly not at this computer, writing this poem that you see
I ain't taking the piss
But if I didn't exist?
Surely I'd be born to a different entity
May be not as me.
Although I must say, that I would have the same facial expression, the same walk, talk smile and style.

When the Creator created this cosmos he had me in mind, down to the first hair that dropped off my head, too the brain cells that produced this poem and not a letter instead. IF; could never be? Just as the Creator chose me. IF; for just a small two letter word, will one day put things in the past, present and future, so in its right context let us just say IF is me.

Unforgettable

Unforgettable; that's what you are
Unforgettable; as far as the moon is from the stars
The days I've loved you, have accomplished its mission
And every situation has resolved its resolution

Heavens eyes have given you a smile
And owing to that reason, you have perfected your style
Unforgettable; and so delightful you are
Unforgettable; you're like a car from the future,
A flying car

Beautiful in dreams and reality,
For my eyes have seen
A girl and an angel without know sin,
That's why I'm so keen
Unforgettable; and truly amazing
Unforgettable; that's all I've been saying

With eyes seductive and lips so pure
Yet having a golden heart and much, much more
Unforgettable; every time you're around me
Unforgettable; that's what you are

Beautiful Ebony Man

With your creative ability, and your smile so clear
Yet your depths touchable and your kindness rare
Though feasible a king, in your past life
It's a certainty to me: I want to be your wife

I compare you to a diamond, cut into a rose
From the most expensive stone, only the
Creator knows
What makes you fascinating is your constant awareness
And your composure or positivity, in times of tiffs

With hands on my heart, I hope you understand
Darling I say I love you, I couldn't wish for a better man
As time toddles on, and together we grow strong
Beautiful ebony man, one thing I do know: we can't go
wrong

Beautiful Ebony Woman

A constant reminder of the things you do
Gives me the incentive to love just you
Collective thoughts images and views
Brings me to the fact that I love you for true

What depth of intricate beauty I see
With a delectable smile so radiant to me
My conscious thought of an aura so sweet
A delightful appearance and a body petite

With a million words to express your smile
So healthy so vibrant inexhaustible style
Contented to know that we were meant
Fascinated by the reality an angel sent

To abide forever my dreams delight
Having you beside me night after night
Combined with health and you always there
Is my day's resolution and my every day prayer.

Beautiful To Me

While looking around me, my sight did behold
A young lady, with eyes more worthy than gold
I must remind you of how beautiful you are
For you're an Ebony woman with eyes like stars

Your eyes a shade of a brown that's bright
A delectable appearance and a body just right
The reminiscence of your smile is like a rose in bloom
Picturesque in style, like the fullest of high moons

I'll describe you as an Angel, while from heaven sent
With a beauty that's transparent and a caring heart that's meant
Everybody is unique in their own special way
But for you my dear, I've got more than a million words to say

You're kind, pleasant, jolly, thought provoking
Your character is conducive to peace, positive creative, sensitive, caring, adorable, admirable, loveable, delectable,
Delightful and beautiful
You're simply the best

Delight

I want to delight you with my joy
To show you that your mind is not just a toy
Encamps you with my love so divine
Make you comprehend that you're mine just mine
What secret do I impart?
To make you know that you're close to my heart
The respect I show is due to you
I've found a friend: I know what to do

I've anticipated this moment: since the stars were wrapped
up in the
Creator's hands,
Way back in the day when ELO said lets
Create man
Its common knowledge that we we're meant to be,
Like you and I understand the concept of birds flying free.
As the mountain peaks reaches up to the sky above:
My heart reaches to your heart for that tender Kind of love

Forty-Two And A Day

As I hear the birds from a new day that dawns
I contemplate this thought, for I m forty-two' and a day,
Will I aspire to all my aspirations?
Or will the years dwindle away in fairy tale ends?
My friend only time can allow me to achieve this goal,
For time conceals the hidden beauty of life,
And life which is beautiful within it self
Is time.

Symbolic Boxer

My defense is your attack,
So your action brings my conspired reaction,
Either way it is our compulsive instincts.
But then again if our action is spontaneous
We may suffer the counter attack of our previous decision,
In other words life is like a good boxer,
Depending on how big your mistake is
You might feel the consequences.

I Swear

As I seek for peace of mind
And search for a woman who is loving and kind
Her ways unfathomable her depths sublime
Yet her knowledge of life from endless times.

When we set eyes on each other we'll click
Like the chimes of a clock in rhythm, we'll go tick tack tick
Whilst with her personality, Very charismatic
Leaving all the more room,
For her to be romantic.

My promise is that I would be positive
Also: I should always make space in my heart, to be sensitive
Just like composing a poem, in our relationship I would be creative
And then we'll give each other, all the more reason to live

In Memory Of Steven Lawrence

Reluctant to give up on a future so bright
Acquainted with grief, yet positivity in sight,
Our motion to embrace, our history and race
Has brought us good fortune, for the future we face.
When all around us things seem so oblique:
Don't be discouraged, for we know we're unique,
From the colour of our skin, to our up tempo heart beat:
For the souls of our ancestors, who wouldn't take defeat.

With a flicker of the picture that tells you the story,
Not: his: story: but our story.
Look into my eyes, for no book can contain our knowledge
From time long ago: I'm talking way back you know
Beyond the days of slavery
We were versed in the arts of astrology, chemistry even
human biology. Then for many years a history taken,
Devastating effects even on the latter generations,
Warriors reduced to corpses, when they refused to comply:
Wives would see their children sold when others would buy

Looking back and seeing the future unfold: It gives me
great pleasure to see our ebony children's dreams and goals
Yet times will change as our story is told, from here to
eternity

Be strong and be bold-Take Steven Lawrence a prime example for you and me. But among us it's significant to know, that there must be unity.
Before I go one thing I want you to know, please it's imperative.
Look into your mirror today and see your ancestors, For they never went away!

Including Every Race

A slave to man, is his life at hand,
But beyond the grave, is eternity's land

While confined to this world,
Our knowledge grows,
Yet with man's departure,
Only the Creator knows.

As I look at the ways of human nature,
How man has strayed,
From the laws of his Creator,

Rejecting his oracles and original plans,
When saying that all man comes from monkeys,
And not the Creator's hands.

OH that all men would have a common goal, and have faith
To groom their children in the righteous paths,
And to include every race

Just A Dream

As I find myself pondering over a certain dream
The reality of such I've never seen

My decision to obtain a thought such as this
Has brought me this moment, I'm closer to her kiss

As I confront my fears she's always there
Telling me to be positive and have no fear

She's my déjà vu
The fusion of my parallel worlds for true

Patiently I wait for the coming of that date
While I watch the hands of time with a longing faith

Can a dream be turned into a reality seen?
Or is a dream just a dream: to those that dream.

Life And Society

As I drive myself to write and write
I consider all the sleepless nights

Worthy the pain of all the toiling
For one day I know this will be my living

When I formulate the words that are seen so clear
Convincing words that are plucked from the air

Guarded by my sensitive mind
While culminating fact from endless times

As I survey the world of my mind so deep
And climb the mountains high and steep

I've acknowledge the pit falls, gullies and holes
And all the soldiers that have lost their souls

I have not began to experience, the full capacity of my mind
Yet I know with experience that it will come in time

As I seek and search for a knowledge so grand
I include the Creator in my master plans

But it's not all about me; it's about life and society
How man has forgotten the very meaning of democracy

In every country moral standards has fallen below average
Mankind in his ways has become beast like, and even savage

We justify all the nature of our bad deeds,
What kind of life are we leaving to our up and coming seeds?

When will get it right?
Stop the wars stop the bloodshed; stop the hypocrisy stop the greed

Living Without You

I have scaled the mountain high and steep
I've walked the valley wide and deep
Yet nothing can I find, but distortion and crime
And all humanity: living off of borrowed time

Though dazzled by the man of words
I look beyond the words I've heard
For to give me inspiration, and to set my heart pulsating
And the joy, of the Creator speaking through his creation

Living with you is like an eclipse of the sun
Because before light was created, you and darkness was one
Scientist are baffled by your creative power
Knowing one second one minute, his life could be over: in that very hour

Conspirer to understand, that I would never put my trust in the hands of anybody but the Creator
For man is fathomable
But the Creator is unfathomable

Lonely Eyes

Compelled to remember her beautiful eyes,
A laugh, a smile, when I clock the depths: even a sigh,
While related to sadness I feel her pain,
Yet in the mirror of her eyes, I smile just the same:
Why, when, how, why you
When we talked we discussed our deepest concerns,
Two fragile minds, lost but about to turn.
Difficult to disguise the pain inside,
Our appetite grows for the words of the wise
Why, when, how-why you.

Mother

A kind of love I've never seen
With a devotion to her children so strong and keen

My mother absorbs the love I feel
For my father who has passed on, from this realm so real

In question: I feel a void within my soul
For a soldier gone on, who lived till he was old

As I capture those visions of the nights passing times
I think of my father and how he was kind

My mother grew me up to love the Almighty
To have understanding and always show mercy

May she continue to live and have a long life?
For she's a woman of substance and a devoted wife

My Love

Can you taste the energy or her serene ability?
Like a chef that has mastered a thousand recipes,
As soft as my darlings breasts,
As we caress the words that are hard to digest,
Words, which are of truth so eloquent,
Darting images of a love that's sent.
Who am I talking about?
That of a woman whose beauty will never decompose.

Hold Firm

If we confiscate this impulse and reach for the sugar,
Will the dish be sweet to the taste with a harsh aroma?
Yet this thought is tempting for sugar is real sweet,
But let this thought be taken down to the abyss,
For that which is sweet also, has sharp teeth.
Who am I talking about?
Losing your lady for a sweet smelling
Stinging nettle of a woman.

MY Way

A slave to write at the pace I do
Each page each line, which is done through and through
My abilities concern is the harmony I yearn
For those words made perfect and all done in tune
Confronted with words which seem such a maze
Diluted with thoughts given by words exchange
While plucked from the air with divine ability
A sense of style drawn by my agility

It's not my public announcement to agree
Yet the work I do excites not only me
When my work is finished I've solved an equation
And it is there I seek for a grander solution
Poetry to my heart has driven me a wedge
From all the other obstacles that's kept me on edge
The simplicity of things like, I love you
To the depths and degrees concerning you and me

I have always believed that one can achieve
Work towards your goals and neglect your dreams
Aspire to a level beyond which you can achieve
While holding fast to the reality of your dreams

Our Last Days

Our destiny has but one last end
To meet those of our long lost friends

You will find comfort in the fact that it's just the beginning
Where; the inner man or inner woman takes over and life
has no ending.

Collective images of the past reunited
While the future not yet mapped: though partially sighted

Engraved in our minds was our life once before
With few opportunity's and many closed doors.

Yet time will change as the other side we reach
For the Creator will be there with open arms to greet

Let's not be deluded in the facts that appear
In the life after death he will always be there.

Reclaim

My faith yet dwindling, I must reclaim
In my search for my Creator once again
By conscious consent I left his side,
A devastating effect, as I watch the ocean tide.

Blinded by the many voices, I chose to choose none
For everybody claims; that their God is the chosen one.
So as I channel my thoughts from deep within
I draw from the resources of righteousness and not from sin
Yet I know that I have to make an amend
For the Creator who I so love, and who is my best friend

The Creator

Before time was, he was and still is,
For time cannot conceal the fact that he exists
Superior to man:
His foundations is in the heaven the sea and the dry land,
Yet his hand is in the heart
Of those who love him and understand

Rekindling A Flame

Rekindling a flame that was once on hold
I speak form the heart and not from what I've been told
When we meet again, how will our relationship be?
Will we be friends or will we be lovers that have been
Set free?

When I consider her ways, I was a fool to leave her side
For a thousand years or more I wish I could abide
As a rose that is guarded by its thorns
I should have taken her under my wings, and from all the
storms

Reflecting on the time we spent together
Looking back I know she's a proud baby mother
We all go through life's ups and downs and stress
Mine was that I never loved anybody at the right time I
guess

I liken her eyes unto a starry full moon night
Her lip to a million precious gems so bright
Her body, like the sun hurrying for the daylight
A prescription for love is her delight

Rekindling a flame that was once on hold
I speak from the heart and not what I've been told
When we meet again, how will our relationship be?
Will we be friends, or lovers that have been set free?

Stop And Think

Greetings to those of you, who have a passion for poetry,
My ambition is to fascinate our minds,
With things that will happen to you and me,
Stop and think, let us analyze our condition
And think about our, dreams and aspirations,
Now think about the things that will give us satisfaction,
It is a dream and aspirations?
Imagine a bridge and at the beginning of the bridge
We are born-yet the bridge has no end,
According to the average life span
Where are we on the bridge my friend?
Stop and think have we aspired anything
Towards our dreams and aspirations?
Although we are resilient
We need to make a start on our fundamental foundation.
In analyzing our condition, we have the mental blue
To our dreams and aspirations,
Yet it is the gap In between,
Where we have to fulfill our dreams and destination
Stop and think, what is needed to enhance our ability to
achieve, Is quality time, peace of mind:
Someone to love and also to be loved
So close your eyes and stop and think

Sunrise From East To West

As the crack of dawn begins to appear
The star's that once shone so bright, slowly disappear
And the birds, welcome the day ahead
While the worms, seek for their daily bread

Although the sun rises from the east, and sets in the west
This day just begins and it's hard to imagine the rest
From slumber from sleep: a human being wakes
While some are drawn away from this world to the undertakers

People getting ready, to start the day in all different ways
Some bowing down on their knees, to the Almighty in praise
Others marking the Lottery, to see what they can raise
Yet on the other hand some wait on the dole, because that's the way they get paid

Crime raises its ugly head once again
Another kid dead in the ghetto, what a crying shame
Politicians campaigning for a better way of life
Yet the issues they suggest don't concern you and I.
Mans problems all started with his inability to agree
For if we would all compromise a little,
We would be sure to have some sort of harmony.

Symbolic Wind

Poised to achieve our goals which is beyond the stars,
While reluctant to look back for sudden change of atmospheric winds,
For this wind is a phenomenon, it will not blow you off course,
But sucks you within itself,
Then it will show you your destination, while you're going in the opposite direction.

A Delicate Rose

Like drops of rain that breaks forth on a garden rose,
For growth that is inevitable, there my heart goes.
When I held you in my arms so delicate yet tight,
My thoughts was though time was created,
You were created as a light,
So keep on shining bright.

Cry Freedom

When the cage is closed the bird will sing,
As the cage is opened the bird will fly,
So I'm not about to chop off its wings,
For then I know, it will surely die.

The Animal Kingdom

You've seen me locked up behind a cage so small
Confined to this space and being gaped at by all
I once was called the king of the jungle
Now I'm treated as some kind of mongrel.
Lions are known for their hunting,
That's what they do
Not kept locked up, as some kind of spectacle in a zoo
I long for the nature of the African plains
To see the gazelles and to find my range.
Prisoners are locked up because they'd have committed a crime
Think of the injustice of me doing time
What would it be like if I was suddenly set free?
It would be hard to cope, for I'm use to captivity.
Though I dream of my land beyond the far away seas
And think of all the other animals that are caged like me
Unlike man we animals have never considered suicide
Yet man-to-man they even contemplate genocide.
Back in my country, I see people dying of a thing they call
Aids: it affects the immune system, and brings on the appearance of old age
The Americans have medication that will prolong the lives of Aids victims in Africa
Yet it comes with a price they can't even barter
You may ask me how I know this
I'm the king of the jungle, it's my duty not to hit and miss.

The Pains Of War

It amazes me how man has gone so far with technology
Yet their attitude to life has become so greedy
We have war in the Middle East over oil
Then war between the Jews and the Palestinians because of soil

The difference between Bin-laden and bush
Is bush is a legalized terrorist under the hush
Voted in illegally before the votes went through
And having control over America and even me and you

The American public suffered through the twin towers disaster
Yet the Americans protested against the war, because what would happen after
Millions of people all over the world took to the streets
Yet Blair and bush would have no such defeat

They also spent billions in funding the war
People who believed in democracy their hearts they tore
Before they put all their efforts into catching Bin-laden
They took another route, and went after Hussein and his Men
Bloodshed has taken on a new toll
And the majority of youth don't live till their old,

Because of this strange wave, gun crime has gone on the increase
Suddenly there's no letting up to allow peace

We have to focus on a new way of teaching our youth
Bringing them up in strong moral understanding and truth
Teaching them in war no side is right
It's time for unity it's time to stop the fight.

The Child Laments

I've seen many a beautiful things, before you wake up,
I see the rising of the sun; everywhere where you are I'm there,
You need me that I swear I've seen you nice,
I've seen your atrocities I've seen you smile,
I've even seen the unlawful killing, of that young child's parent,
What am I?
I'm a door,
You use to lock up those who you choose,
Yes,
I'm a simple door,
That can tell you,
Much-much
More.

The People's Choice

As I draw from the intricate parts of my brain
I contemplate this thought that I must retain
Imagine a world free from war and pain,
Where people's views could be heard and no restrained.

There must be a solution to the world affairs,
Why one set of people live around riches and another tears,
Celebrate with me a future that will set us free from fear,
Yet in all this show humanity that YOU real care.

We speak of democracy: yet the people have no voice,
Politicians have taken away their right and even their choice,
It's time to stand up and make some noise,
And think of the future of our girls and boys

To My Ancestors

As we soar across the sky and clouds,
My friend to me I'm Ebony and proud.
While we look into the mirror of our mind,
Focus and you will find royalty of a kingly kind.

Conscious images of Ebony which is beauty,
Defined as power and abundant spirituality.
Hide not the facts but give us our history,
For it's in all Ebony people's interest
To know their destiny.

What More Can I Say About Life

Success is not seen in the amount of money you have
But it is how happy you've made your life,
Whereas success: can also be measured in contentment.
We can determine our future by what we've done in the past, with our past mistakes we can learn by them, and develop a better understanding of one self

Contained in our minds should be a reason to better our self's,
Never give up on opportunities:
For some opportunities come but once.
The secret of life is to measure your distance, search for your goal and go for it,
In reaching your goals: neglect not to think where you came from

Always abide by the principles of moral understanding,
For in life you will find
That what goes around sometimes comes around.

When confronted with fear don't tackle them head on: develop a strategically plan that can be scrutinized by your friends, then double check.

What should I say about nature, may the indigenous people
of all countries enjoy the labor of their first fruits.
Hero's are created of men with courage, while its also
courageous not to go to war: for the sake of saving lives.

Although we spend the majority of our lives as adults, a
fraction of our lives was spent as children,
So when dealing with children:
Be reminded that we were once young.
While we have made this environment for our children, let
us pray they see our mistakes and conform to a better way
of life, that their days may be long on the earth.
As for the scientist that spend their time making bombs of
mass destruction, may they be confounded and their
foolishness turned into wisdom, for the healing of all
nations.

It should never be an option to gather facts, for in obtaining
knowledge we are educating ourselves for future events.
What more can I say about life,
Consider the toil of a mother and the labor of a father,
Because the joy of good parents is liken unto riches untold.

Yazmin

As time presses on, I write this poem as if
I'm writing a song
For I wish you were here in my arms,
Telling me nothing can go wrong

While time penetrates the night air
The saddest story of my life,
Is you not being there

For your heart was salvaged form a wreckage so deep
That it left you with compassion and a nature so sweet

Darling I tell you I truly believe
That you can be who you want to be: and achieve all of
your dreams

The true love that we seek for, is not just a dream
But it's the reality we yearn for, from the future for seen

Who Am I

To pose a question, help me to think?
Though many are killed, justice is the link,
Imagine a people no colour of skin,
Where everybody is judged by their contents within,
This is designed for those who agree,
Utopia the future we all want to see.

Though proud to be the colour we are,
This system has failed us, no justice by far,
Equality I shout the reason I do,
For lack of a better word, I put to you,
What beauty this world has to possess,
Come on, let's put racism to the test
And give it a rest.

Death becomes common among those who are poor
Remember I'm saying...no more, no more
Disgusted by the ways of today,
Few are rich and the majority on low pay
There must be something we can do,
If not me, then you ...and you

First World War One and then World War Two,
If there's any more killing,
Should it be me or will it be you,
Together let's look beyond today,
Let's look to the future for a different way
The signs are here for us to see,
Come join my quest for us to be free
Who am I, but me?

Two Sides Of A Coin
By
Dermoth A. Henry

Sophisticated in the art of writing,
Makes me feel like I've experienced a sighting
This is not my usual topic,
But somebody has to write about it.
Now a chemical imbalance in the brain,
Is mostly classified as mentally insane,
But there is an advantage I must confess,
I'm starting to write poetry at my best.

Leaving school with no education,
In the hope one day that I'll reach the nations,
A voice to be heard from station to station,
Educating the nation with good information.
I'm not satisfied with my situation,
But I'm not going to cry I want to die,
Or putting my hand in another man's till,
Then telling everybody I'm feeling ill.

With a smile on my face that's hard to erase.
Sometimes I feel down but isn't that a phase.
I believe it affects the whole human race
I guess I've changed I'm not the same,
I don't feel bad or have any one to blame.
Because I remember going insane.

Logic will tell you it's not a good thing.
But something good must come from within.
If you're mentally ill don't feel dismayed,
There's a lot we can do to change our ways.
I've learnt that whatever condition we're in.
We must be on top and we must win

When You're Low

When you think nobody really cares
The Creator will always be there
And when people despise you
The Creator will compel,
Them to love you.

You see you're like a rose in a garden
Transparent beautiful and kind.
People many not realize it
But you're a mother full of creative tips.
Give me a second and I'll tell you why
When you were conceived the river beds ran dry,
And the sky folded in on itself
And created a shelf
And there you stepped down from the heavens above,
With love for your children and all humanity.

Currently I'm thinking that I should look after you,
Until we're old and grey and have nothing to say.
Whatever you're going through fight it,
For the day will come when we rejoice because we've
Come out of the pit
Your boys will turn around and show you so much love;
And you'll be overwhelmed as if two angels fell from above.
This isn't poem it's a message!!

Resources

Natural resources
Diamonds; mostly found beneath the ground
Oil; found in the ocean or seas
Pearls; found among water

Gold; dug up or found in shallow water
Man has made these a necessity
Or has man, become just greedy
You take from the Earth
Yet you don't give back its worth

The tsunami; Hurricane Katrina were all caused by man
Playing with natural resources
There's enough on the Earth to keep man occupied
Yet dem seh dem a go a moon fi ride

As precious as life is
When I look at mine I don't look at his
But I always remember how he fell.

Phenomenon

To enter the mind of visions and signs: Is just a thought away,
Yet insight that pertains to the intricate brains
Is ignited and somehow sustained.

The flirtation of thoughts
That's captured those visions,
Rockets to the moon:

Computers, robots even televisions,
Were all brain waves of Immaculate Conception?
Far beyond deception.

We're living high tech
So don't try to neglect

The phenomenon you miss
You might just regret

Love Story

People love for different reasons
Some for the sensation of the season
Others for the palate and the occasion

Given to understand, why a man loves a woman
Is something I can comprehend, first the man's attracted to the woman
Then to the aisles, they go both hand in hand

It is said that a woman's love has no boundaries
And a man's heart transparent, you should see,
Yet like children there should be no negativity.

Different is the road to love
But when we reach it, it is that which is sent from above
People also say there is no such thing as 50/50 love
Is that coming from your lover or from the other?

Look At Me Now

To pose a question, help me to see?
How you see me, the way I see me
I try to be nice, and I want to be polite
But even then I have to struggle day and night.

As time passes by, I long to be a better person
Clean up my act, stay on track
And get good feedback
But the hardest things for me to do, is be me
Knowing that being me is being totally free.

Now I find myself not trusting anymore
And you know what I'm doing better for sure
If I knew it was that easy
I never would have tried to be somebody else, but me.

Fact of Nature

Beyond boundaries beneath, white capped snow
Lays a heart that's warm only the Creator knows.
The twigs of a tree, the imagination of bees churning out honey
To please you and me

I'm reminded of an eclipse,
That's sent the moon before the sun,
Understand that time has a way, its course it must run. And the constant heat of the tropical terrain
Knowing that when April comes it's, sure to bring rain.

Developed in the womb
A baby sleeps sound
But once removed from the womb, they need, must cry aloud

Speak if you have a reason
Or hold your peace,
For the tarantula has a venomous bite
And also sharp teeth.

Growth Of Ages

Tiny feet pitter- patter
When you're young nothing matters
Happy Birthday special day
Greetings my child you're one today

At the age of three, you know what you need
To go to school,
And learn to read.

Six weeks holidays
France, Gibraltar or maybe Majorca
Different stages, growth of ages
You're learning fast
You'll soon collect wages.

Leaving school a change of environment
Having a job is one of the requirements
Delighted for once, the joy of a young lady
Together as one with the hopes of a baby.

Tiny feet pitter- patter
When you're young nothing matters
Happy day special day
Let's greet another child that's on the way.

Guidance

Oh beneficial one: who created not only me but also all that I see around me. As I dare to open my mouth, knowing that I'm but a mere human being: give me the utterance to speak words of wisdom, as I attempt to understand your unfathomable vast omniscient power. Open my eyes to see that which was hidden from the foundation of the world, so that it may be unveiled not only to me, but also to all those around me. I know that it is once appointed unto a man to die: and after that cometh the judgment, so while a man is alive and he commits sin, he isn't judged but chastised in order for him to correct his faults. Oh merciful one I have been chastised many times, yet why won't I take heed, help me to surrender my will to you, for my knowledge concerning you is as a mere speck of sand in the Sahara desert. As I seek your guidance for today, give me due cause to be obedient: for what would it profit me if I obtain all the things I have ever dreamt of, and lose the companionship of the Creator, knowing that He who is my companion, shall one day be my judge.

Holy Communion Age 8

Quinton: You're a child of wonder
You're a child of grace
And you have that of an angel's face
Speedily as you come of age
And life is set before you, like a stage

May you grow up to be a man
That nothing in this life can faze
While I know in life, the Creator will protect you
This I know, so will daddy Richard too

Q-Quality of person
U-Unique in character
1-Intelligent boy
N-Never giving up •
T-Truthful and honest
0-On the ball
N-Number one son

Lots of love Richard - Psalms 1

Dermoth's Story

I've been mentally ill now for 37 years, the transaction from being healthy to having mental ill health has been a short lived one. I'm now 56 years old and I've spent most of my life under the diagnosis of bi-polar effective disorder.

Medication is supposed to stabilize me but I've always believed that although I take full responsibility for my actions, the medication would also determine what actions I would take. Because I believe that every substance that isn't naturally grown will have side effects.

I must admit since becoming mentally ill, I have exercised my brain well. By my taking up poetry I've become more expressive in my day to day experiences.

Classified as:
Mental illness is a journey
Sometimes you're on your bending knees
When falling down
Is hard to pick yourself off the ground
But one thing in life
You should never stick around
On the ground

Dreams And Aspirations

I have always wanted to be tailor
I guess according to that dream, I'm a failure
Now I've taken up poetry
It's put my life, in some sort of normality

I speak from my heart, the things I feel
And from the journey I've taken, I keep it real
To tell the truth I've never looked back
Because I think my life's on track

As a profession, would I go back to tailoring?
Yes. I would, I have always been creative in designing
For life is about fulfilling your dreams and aspirations
And fulfilling your dreams and destinations.

Why

Some people love, things they can't see
And others love things they can't touch
But creator why me, why me, how come I love you so much?

When I divide the pain I've been through
It's more gain just to love you
Why doesn't man understand that the creator
Has his hand in everything that man plans

The highest form of machinery is the brain
So why do we abuse our power to function
And become hell bent on destruction
Look how man has distorted creation
Digging the soil for oil, diamonds and steel is bound
To cause corruption

You can't take out natural resources and expect
Things to stay the same
There's got to be a change, there's got to be a change,
There's got to be a change.

Your Hair

I identify you, as a rose before the storm
And your beautiful hair out of the norm.
As I gather more momentum, and think about your beauty
You're an ebony woman, with clear identity

Men will love you, for who you are,
Not for what you possess,
Because of a truth, the Creator made you the best.
There's something about you, that everybody loves your style, your agility and your peace, like a dove

When the Creator created you,
The heavens ruptured and the Sun shone through.
And that's why the Creator loves you.

Notice how your hair's starting to grow,
And all men look at you, you know
It's time to claim your beauty,
This isn't a wish, it's your duty.

Violent World

Coast to coast
Deaths and murder
Young and old

None to quail
This violent hell
Just tortured youths
Deaths twisted smell

Criminal's crimes unsolved
Life's dimensions overthrown
Yes; Cain's home

Men, kill for
Others, love for
Some, live for
Money, evils core
What justifies killing
No pricey treasure
Life's for living

Dermoth's Love For Belzie

Mum; how I'm compelled to think of you
The way you was, to your words so true
Deny me not a word and mum I'll tell you why
Despite your death, I can't say I haven't tried.

I've fallen down so many times
Yet brushed myself off, it comes in like a nursery rhyme
Though life has a way of playing tricks
I know to the ground, I'll never stick

Bruised and battered, like a pear out of shape
I felt your deaths blow, although it came late
I'm also writing this in a poetic form
So I can try to weather, my mind before the storm
Mum; beyond the grave you speak to me loud
Telling me to separate myself from evil, and be strong and proud
But how can I be strong, without my father's hand
For he too has gone too far underground.
Let the Creator bless me, in my search in this land
And happiness be accepted, as it is given to man.

Queen Of Hearts

As beauty engraves her delightful face
Yet her body so delicate and full of grace
Though time contracts the space between us
She's the woman in my life; she's worth all the fuss

If I'm talking about you, then you will know
For you're one of the reasons, why I'll never let you go
Real to my heart as you kiss my lips
I know it's not a game, of hit and miss

A phenomenal response when we fell in love
As if the heavens opened up, while the stars fell from above
Before I met you, I contracted the common cold
Suffered from a fever and the flu
But it wasn't just because of you
To fall in love, my time on earth; was over due

The more I think, of how life should be
Just how nature's put us together naturally
Has baffled, amused and even silenced me
Because we're so fortunate to be loved and love so free.

Unedited

What can I do but thank you for being you?
The inspiration of my love for poems,
You made me express things that lay
Dormant from my inception until the
Reality of my dreams.
I must confess that in the corner of my mind,
My thoughts runs on you most of the times.

Consistent the way I express my words to you,
Still I pray my love is true,
To tell the truth and not deny,
Before meeting you, I've never wrote poetry about love or even tried.
Yes I count myself blessed that my poetry
Is getting good better best.

Down to you this fact is true,
My concept of love is because of you.
As I extract from my minds eyes,
Your beauty, which is pure with no disguise,
Then confronted by your reaction
With just one phone call,
Brings me to the satisfaction that say's it all,
I love you.

New Day

Three hundred and sixty-five days a year
Without you my darling, there would be many a tears
If I chose to be alone, I wouldn't make my house a home
Because instead, you've given me marrow for my bones

Joobs I love you, I couldn't wish for another
For my love for you surpasses any other
Can the mountains withhold the snow from its tops?
As the grass is green, Joobs you're my lot

Heaven has given me a bride to be
And Joobs; I'm so proud that you love me
As we spend time together and go through stormy weather
May our delight be, only in each other?

Finally I say, loves been good to me
Because I've been to the east and I've been to the west
But sweetheart, you're all those things that life knows best

As I round off my words
It's something you've never heard
So I'm going to put it in a parable
To make you know that I'm durable

Love is like a seed that takes time to grow,
Not a seed that breaks forth in spring and dies in winter,
But it has the traits of an old oak tree.
Thank you Joobs for loving me

How Are You Hurting

Human frailty acknowledged
Deaths simplicity sighted
Common goals ahead

Social degradation upheld
Leaders led astray
Money distracts minds
Immoralities complacent times

The legacy left
The trying children
The barbaric history

Youths crying justice
Is this it?
Open heart surgery
Conscious moral awareness

Process of delivery
Join the quest
Society pleads it

Our Journey To Success

Subjected to the ordeal of life,
Gives me all the more Courage to strive,
I want to experience wealth, it's not wrong
To experience wealth and physical health,
But would want make me want, to want more.
I don't want to win the lottery,
I would like to work hard for my children and me.

It is expedient that I grasp success,
Because Poverty has become something hard to digest,
While life in the ghetto is full of unrest,
Even young children are suffering from high levels of stress,
Look at the amount of people that are
Dying of heart attacks or they would call it cardiac arrest,
It makes you wonder if life is just a big test,

We must all contain ambitions,
For in life we all come across different situations
Yes it is that, that will determine our destination.
We all have the capability to disagree,
Yet our fundamental decision in life is
To seek and search to be free.

You're Heaven Sent

Highly recommended as an angel of beauty
Is my true confession, and also my duty
To say the least, you're truly unique
And your smile has, a way, of making my heart skip a beat

A delight to compare you, to the morning sunrise
When I subconsciously look right into your eyes
With a spectacular breath taking sight to behold
Your body more precious than the finest of gold

With a queen of such beauty, I have to admire
For the Creator has blessed me, with whom I desire
While taking a look, you're unquestionably poised
And for that my darling, the heavens erupted and the angels made noise

If I could count the stars above
I would undoubtedly start with you my love
For your heaven sent, you're an angel meant
Yet with you my dear, 1will always be content

Beautiful

Conveyed in my mind is a girl so divine
Who to me has a love that is one of a kind
From day light to moon-----
She reminds me of the fact that she is truly----

While love draws us closer and binds us-------
May we be joined at our hearts and our love last----
Select if you will a path we must -------
Then I'11 walk you down the road1 until we get -----
It's positive to know that you love me----
As I've gained experience, from all that you've done and --

May the trials of life bring us closer-------
And strengthen our hands in times of stormy ---------
As I listen to your words and I hear your --------
I think of an angel, with many words of--------

{VOICE) (SHINE) (WED) {FOREVER) (TOGETHER)
(KNOW) (SO)
{TOGETHER) (CHOICE) (TREAD) {WEATHER)
{MINE)

How Can One Be Happy

Having patients is one of the ways to obtain happiness.
Open heart is a sacrifice, which is experienced from within.
We all know happiness is contentment, that's what it brings

Contained in my heart is a joy that brings a perfect peace.
Another way of expressing peace is in depth and tranquility.
Never the less it all boils down to, a sincere kind of love.

Opportunities always comes, a man will find someone to love
No I'm not an expert; love has a way of appearing.
Encourage yourself; be yourself because I want to be me too.

Beneficial is the person that waits, for love comes to everybody.
Evaluate your happiness, scrutinize your timing and wait.

Having appreciated what you have, it's like flowing waters.
Apparently all rivers run to the sea, and the sea has depths
People miss understand love, instead of embracing it they run
Peculiar we humans, how one can have loved someone so deep
Young people love each other that is what makes us unique.

Unseen Danger

Why when the end I would near,
The unseen danger would suddenly appear.
A Degree of insanity for one to bear,
Is much, much pain and many a tear.
Impartially impaired,
The brain so severe,
It's not something I condone,
It's something I fear.

The things I regret so plain to see,
All things done good just couldn't be me.
With no time on my side, how could I win?
The brain so oppressed, and divided within.
If I could reverse time, my mission would be,
To embrace the emotions that, were feeble to me.

The path I remember so clear long ago,
The mind unbruised with time to lose.
My mind has lapsed into a gear unknown,
Had it been first, I would know there was a third.
Let me explain the thoughts I feel,
I want to be me,
I want to be free.

Things that I find so beneficial to me,
Have slipped my grasp, and now gone free.
All my work has time erased,
Articulated knowledge unfathomable to see
Gone, gone just couldn't be me.
What secret things do I desire?
Not to fall from grace,
But to be closer to Him who is Higher.

Completely oblivious my smile once so sweet
With feet on the ground I stood so neat.
When looking from a distance, I'm physically unique,
But when mind in turmoil, I'm truly oblique.
Just a mirage of someone incomplete.
I hope to know the master's plan,
Give me now and I will understand.

Bitter this world has become to me,
Obstruction, frustration in all liberty.
What fraction of sleep would I care to have?
Sleep taken away by fears of nightmares.
To grasp the future and what it would hold,
I'd have to be strong and I'd have to be bold.

Sometimes I consider my life to be.
Lost in my mind of unconscious deeds.
With no control of my actions if be but far beyond my capacities and needs.
And an impulse that brings reactions you see
Inexcusable behavior, a mental disorder.
Depression by name.
Bi-polar by nature.

Options

Then again you will never know
A sweet smelling stinging nettle,
Until you meet a flower that has
Growth worthy of petals,
I know the question you're asking
Is where do I look? The answer is
Fate will bring you together like the
Pages of a book.
What am I talking about?
Wisdom lies at the door of your heart,

And beyond that door is her heart,
Let her in

What Comes Next?

As she lay undoubting on the bed,
Because finally we got together and we were wed
Her hair platted to one side,
Legs spread as she waited for the guide
With noted feelings inside,
Two virgins ready to give away their pride.

Words symbolically uttered,
Yet soft to the ear and Bentalawah to the eye.
What comes next?
As I enter the Bentalawah cave, and feel the old graves,
Step aside you've had your chance, make way.
She replies; all those that had you, shall flee like fly's
For your guaranteed foreskin is mine.
Don't be blinded by what you see
For I choose you and you choose me.

Happy Valentine's Day

When the Creator created flowers he thought of you,
Like a blue rose protected by its thorns,
Waiting for the morning dew.

Angel's gathered, when your mother gave birth,
Then you appeared SOPHIE, with all a woman's worth.
Deny me not a word and I will tell you why?
Though many have tried to win your heart,
You chose me, and for that I would die.

The song of my heart, is that we will never part,
And may our years be full, with a lot of laughs.
May the secret of your heart be unfolded to me,
As the ships need the ocean, yet the sails need the wind.
To me you're my wife my lover and my best friend.

If the moon should tumble down from the sky,
And the sun itself, should die,
While my love for you, would find some room in the heart,
That proclaimed I do
When I quantify my words so deep, I'm not one to give a big speech
But I do know that the circumference of my heart has been enlarged,
By your love.

Lots of love

Happy Valentine's Day

SOPHIE

Life Doesn't End There

I had a messed up education,
Went to school with many nations
I was going around like I was slick the dick
It turns out years later I got sick, sick, sick
I was going insane my head felt heavy and my feet felt light,
Man I could sleep, man I could sleep all day and night.
Well it got so frightening, I'm talking like thunder and lightning.
The day went by within a twinkling of an eye; it got so bad I couldn't even cry,
But then I fell on my feet
I am so unique, I'm unfathomable, impossible damn near improbable.
When it comes to life, I'm like a dog with a bone, I get all shook up, but I find my way home
Late at night when it's hard to sleep, I get down on my knees to the creator I weep

Can you imagine that: As the intra for those of you who didn't hear the title
Life doesn't end there
I'm talking about life after mental health doesn't have to end there
So the second part of my poem goes like this:

As I look back and check the clock on the wall
I've seen many a fool's rise and fall
I'm like a devastating masterpiece and grand finale
Specializing in poetry and the love of my family
Give me the chance to delight your soul,
I'm here to speak to the young and the old.
Now my papa gone on and my mum gone on.

But the thing they taught me is always, be strong.

Shaheda Is

If I could describe love, by the falling of a star
Then Shaheda, I'm moved by far
For your intellect surpasses that of any subject
Conjugal to this, my earthly planet

How can I fathom, your beauty that is set before me
Only by telling you, that you've done a great job in setting her free
This inner guidance, has allowed Linda freedom I want to tell you that I love you, but I'm left dumb
May be the powers that be, will make you see
A dream
A vision

If a rose could shed, a thousand petals
The fragrance wouldn't be as great as one of your smiles
For your petite, neat, complete and even sweet
And you have a great sense of humor, you're surely elite

When the Creator, who has counted every rain drop; that fell from the sky
Turns round and blesses you, you too shall have eternal life, and never die

Credit

I've not begun to tell you the truth,
Yet all my truth is bound up in my youth.
As a young child sickly but wild,
With no ambition just drifting from
Situation to situation,
My quality of life though bearable,
Led me to something that was undesirable,
From bob a job to jewelry shops,
That's right I was on the; rob.

In the class rooms I was more of a joker or the local fool,
To tell the truth I don't remember anything beneficial from school,
My brains was a mess things were hard to digest,
Being in B math's group for two years,
But not remembering a thing that passed through my ears,
Yet I remember things so clear, so why not English, Math's,
And other subjects that were there.

Departing from school under lock and key,
It was there I first experienced captivity,
At the end of many spells I had a breakdown
And perceived how to read,
Because my mind was open to reading,
I know I could do the things that I could succeed in.
It's a terrible analogy to normal life,
Yet this has brought me behind the pulpit for sixteen years,
And will also bring my pen to life.

Ebony History Seventy's Style

People of colour
Mostly good natured
Generally well mannered

Optimistic thou oppressed
Potentially great people
Talents; vastly extreme

Current; evolving changes
Viciously attacking others
Reasons; slave syndrome

Taken from Africa
Sold as slaves
Traded like cattle
War of shades.

Choose Life

Show me empathy, when tears are rolling down my face,
Show me kindness, when in society I have no place,
If I ever slip slide give me balance on either side

When I'm lonely call my phone or come to my address,
when I'm at home
Given a chance I'II prove to you, that I'm human just like
you
Consider my thoughts as I think of you, how you're never
troubled by what life's thrown at you

Someone once said that peace lies beneath
But who wants to die and answer that question why
Certainly not I

For I have the will to survive, and not give myself the
opportunity to die,
But to be old and grey, and in the quantity of words,
Let us be good husband and wives
And choose life.

Gap Years

To satisfy your ego, I'll tell you a story
This my friend, is not a jack a Norrie
But is a tail of things that has happened to me

I lived a life of crime
Came out of jail after doing my time
While inside I saw a sign

Fragmented though it was, it was a life line
Then I tuned to the Creator and found peace of mind
Now I write poetry most of the times

For sixteen years, preached a gospel that wasn't mine
Must admit, had a great time, yeh it was fine
I would go as far as to say, even divine

As doors opened, things started to change and the times became kind
Yet to tell the truth, I've made many mistakes but I guess that was a change of mind
I'd left the church but not the delight of seeing the signs

To satisfy your ego, I've told you a story
This my friend was not a jack a Norrie
But it's a tail of things that happened to me

To Love And To Hold

Like two lovers drowning their sorrows and pains
Of a love that's lost with nothing to gain
Years of a relationship wasted away
Thoughts of reconciliation from day to day

What would it take to pacify this moment?
The heavens to be open and an angel to be present.
We promised that we would take care of each other
Through all kinds of seasons and even stormy weather

Where did we go wrong?
How come this love diminished after so, so long?

Would it be true to say?
It's my fault, for my heart went astray?
When I contemplate the fate that I made
Will I ever find another lover, whom to come to my aid?

Counsel my soul, with words from them which are of old
Can I never find another lover?
bound by those words To love and to hold....